D1453749

20 Lines A Day

Also by Harry Mathews

Fiction

The Conversions
Tlooth
The Sinking of the Odradek Stadium
Selected Declarations of Dependence
Country Cooking and Other Stories
Cigarettes

Poetry

The Ring
The Planisphere
Trial Impressions
Le Savoir des Rois
Armenian Papers: Poems, 1954-1984

20 Lines A Day

Harry Mathews

The Dalkey Archive Press

ISBN: 0-916583-41-4
LC: 87-73070

First paperback edition 1989

Cover photo: John Foley

Partially funded by grants from The National Endowment for the Arts and
The Illinois Arts Council.

The Dalkey Archive Press
1817 North 79th Avenue
Elmwood Park, IL 60635 USA

*Printed on permanent/durable acid-free paper and bound in the United
States of America.*

Preface

Like many writers, I often find starting the working day a discouraging prospect, one that I spend much energy avoiding. Four years ago I was reminded of an injunction Stendhal gave himself early in life: *Vingt lignes par jour, génie ou pas* (Twenty lines a day, genius or not). Stendhal was thinking about getting a book done. I deliberately mistook his words as a method for overcoming the anxiety of the blank page. Even for a dubious, wary writer, twenty lines seemed a reassuringly obtainable objective, especially if they had no connection with a "serious" project like a novel or an essay. For the next year or so I began many writing days with a stint of at least twenty lines, written about whatever came into my head on a pad reserved for that purpose.

As a background to these intermittent annotations of my life, I should mention that at the time I wrote them I was established in Lans-en-Vercors, a French mountain village half an hour outside Grenoble; that I had been living there since 1976 with the writer Marie Chaix and her two daughters, Emilie and Léonore; that I spent considerable time in or near New York, visiting my mother and teaching at Columbia College; that I made frequent short trips to Paris. In addition to family life, two concerns preoccupied me: the completion of my fourth novel, *Cigarettes,* begun in 1978, and the death in 1982 of my closest friend, the French novelist Georges Perec.

September 1987

[3]

The cats, the women, and the lizards have elongated heads. Birds behave very tame, and not only the hotel crumb-hunters: under a streetlamp last night, pale gray ones like starlings flew down onto a branch above my head I could almost touch. (Marie just saw her first hummingbird, not so tame, now you see it now you don't.) This morning is warm, breezy, a little unreal, I'm filled with an unsleepy stupor, as if on a day after strong drugs. My anxiety is dulled but hardly deadened. Yesterday I told myself: perhaps Georges is really dying now, perhaps I'm letting him die. (Marie recalled my saying that it took four full seasons to start getting used to a death.) Maybe the pain of accepting his death is what's "crippling" me, making me blame myself for forgivable inadequacies: yesterday morning, after going back to sleep and only getting up at nine, I persuaded myself that the day was already wasted. Now I've just read* about the "sense of life" that the Greeks had and that we lost, centuries ago—existence itself. It would be enough for me to let myself let myself live. When I was fifteen, I felt the southern sun and sea like a warm, soothing grace in which to let every kind of worry go. As for the "twenty lines a day, genius or not": just do them.

St. Bart's, 3/16/83

*Barthes

When the wind blows hard, you can lock it out, you can let it in but give it no place to go, or you can let it through. The first two ways are suitable for a cold wind; for a hot one, the last is best, unless you like being stifled or being pummeled with heat. There are still disadvantages: when you let the wind through, especially through your bedroom, especially at night, you have to give up in exchange for coolness all hopes of rest. The wind tumbles in, puffing up the curtains, lifting them high enough to reveal a sky whose stars no longer suggest ecstatic calm. The wind blows, the night stares in at you relentlessly, and the day will never come. Lying awake, after you have learned to give up hoping for rest, you begin hoping for day, and then for peace, and then for strength, if not now at least in a foreseeable future: because now you are lying on your bed in utter weakness. Over you moves the tumbling, clattering wind, and although you know that it's only air and holds no real danger for you, you are nonetheless filled with an emotion worse than terror—a knotted, knowledgeable anxiety that comes to feel like the pit and kernel of your life. It is a dismaying conviction that you have neither substance nor consistency nor even the capacity to resign yourself to this sad condition. This awareness is what makes you so weak that you cannot move (except to turn from your left onto your right side and slip your right arm under the pillow); or perhaps your being unable to move simply becomes the proof of what you are aware of. You go on lying there, too wakeful to sleep, too sleepy to take advantage of being awake (or so you not quite honestly tell yourself), you only let the wind continue its noisy work.

St. Bart's, 3/17/83

The cat walked into the terrace and climbed onto Marie's lap. It settled there, alert at first (as twitching ears attested), only gradually assuming the heaviness that seems to surpass a cat's actual weight, as though relaxation brought an exceptional gravitational thrust into play.

Yellow-breasted sugar birds are what make the crescendo hiss around the corner of our bungalow: like a valve being slowly opened and then shut off before the full flow of high-pressure steam has been reached. The hiss disperses in a quick sputter of high notes.

Just above my diaphragm is a knot that won't be loosed. It keeps me hurrying—get your food eaten, get your errand done, get to the beach. There is no point here in hurrying. Light, warmth, moist cruising clouds, expanses of sweetly cool, just-ruffled water are an invitation to take time, to waste it. Time's use here lies in its being wasted. But I keep asking, what's wrong here? What can leading such a life mean? What kind of people can lead such lives? Of course the answers are that anyone can lead such a life (St. Barthes would add to its enjoyability the enjoyment of deciphering that enjoyability), that such a life is supposed to mean nothing beyond itself (it isn't *necessarily* a product of social injustice), that nothing may be wrong here whatsoever except in my own compulsion to find fault, to find significance.

St. Bart's, 3/18/83

It's satisfying to learn the names of birds I've seen—pearly-eyed thrasher, banana quit—but the satisfaction is less intense than the prior craving to know the names. The names themselves are not to blame (I was quite jubilant to hear the words "pearly-eyed thrasher") except insofar as they *are* names: they quickly disappear into the multitude of other names. So there's another trasher; if "tits" exist, why not "quits"? The actual birds remain as mysterious as ever—utterly alive. They're birds and can never be reduced to mere "birds."

A midnight swim, alone, naked, in the presence of stars and a few distant electric lights. The darkness, the sensations of cooler water and cooler air, bring not particular memories—Menton, Majorca, Corfu— but their sum. The feelings the action arouses then come to seem a part of its nature. Erotic, romantic expectation, no doubt, but a more childish excitement as well: The world is all mine.

The cat came back (for food) and sat in my lap. It is a lean but clean animal. It moves like a slow-motion cat. It does not purr, not even when obviously content. Caressing it, I found appealing the fantasy of a woman entirely covered with spotted-gray, short-furred skin.

The weather here, no matter how cloudy it gets, remains essentially sunny. Clouds are always a welcome relief. No matter how much one loves sunshine, its assault here on eyes and skin makes shade delectable. One knows one's tan will have more fuel than it can use.

St. Bart's, 3/19/83

One daffodil, one only, is blooming on the terrace under my office window. Although it's apparently withstanding today's frost, I can't help feeling not only pity for its mistaking the weather but a certain derision—the kind I feel when I pass a beautiful, fast car that has been stopped for speeding. Similar anomalous analogies: the one guest at a party in evening clothes; a fish stranded in a tidal pool;—and when does a dog exhibit that look that can only be read as embarrassment?

It's useful to make yourself try new procedures in class. Because the results are unpredictable, it's uncomfortable, but the insights it provides into the way people (including you) think and behave are precious. Yesterday, the exercise in which designated "writers" read the openings of their stories to their "readers" didn't turn out, for me, to be as usefully frustrating as I had expected: so I was anxious when I asked for comments. At such times the thing to do is keep people talking. In time useful things will be said.

Being told that during a separation it has been possible to attain a distance towards a relationship is more dismaying than being resentfully attacked for inadequacy.

New York, 3/23/83

How do birds arriving in the spring know that the bugs will be out?

The anchovies sit in their eggs, waiting for the penetration of sunlight into their waters. Horses prod the dank fields: not quite sprawling time yet. Eyes peep from burrows; hawks are waiting for those emergences. Blue is paler. Green is only at its beginnings—not for a while the lank tenderness of confident new leaves unrolling.

A man got out of a car and stood at the corner of a street in a very large city. He made a point of noticing what was natural there. He was chilled by wind, touched by sunlight; he was breathing air, even if the air was cluttered with social smells and substances. (He thought: I could be standing at a country crossroads with a just-fried sandwich in my hand and a smoky tractor passing.) As for the other things, they were natural, too, except that he had to start thinking of nature as human nature. What better kind of nature was there than that? If the place had a problem, it was one of the focus of perception. The overall view— expanses of tar, cement, and masonry—was fine, and details no less so: cracks in stone closely looked at, the intensity of frying oil considered by itself, the tinkle from someone else's headset. What was disap- pointing were middle-distance appearances. There the senses were struck by squalor: ruin, decay, stridency, bad taste, the human nature of humans wounded, sick, old.

New York, 3/25/83

Billy has the staggers again. When he stands up, he wobbles, ever so slightly (he's doing what he can to keep it from showing); when he walks, he takes short steps, looking slowly from side to side; when he stands still, he prefers to lean against something—a wall, a chair, a friend. His condition has nothing to do with drinking, or at least not with being drunk, although it might be an aftereffect.

Billy's a nice man, and he knows it, but he can't accept that he's all right the way he is. He needs, apparently, a daily ration of dissatisfaction with himself. This can take the mild form of badmouthing himself; at other times it will appear as depression or bodily pain, a backache, for instance. It isn't clear whether or not the staggers are another manifestation of Billy's restless self-disgust. He's been having them off and on for years. Recently he's started thinking of them as a harbinger of old age, remembering his father's dizzy spells, which were often accompanied by a loss of memory.

Billy's O.K.—he looks O.K., he acts O.K., he just doesn't feel O.K. At least some of the time. He compares himself to the portrait of Dorian Gray, except that, according to him, he carries the actual portrait somewhere inside him—perhaps, I suggested, engraved on the inner skin of his eyelids? He did not understand what I meant.

New York, 3/28/83

What Billy didn't realize last Monday was that it was the anniversary of his father's death: the third. The first anniversary had brought insomnia and dark-night-of-the-night inspiration (concerning, of all things, masturbation: he still hasn't been able—he still hasn't tried—to establish the connection between masturbation and his father, dead or alive). The second anniversary brought a recrudescence of grief reinforced by and reinforcing the overwhelming loss of his best friend. This anniversary has brought forgetfulness—clearly the worst possible poisoned gift. Forgetfulness means neither acceptance nor indifference. It means death itself: the part of Billy's life that was his father's has now died in him. This may account for the melancholy he has been experiencing, and his getting his bag full of valuable and cherished things smashed under a car wheel.

But what can you expect after all of Billy Bodega? Alone, he frets. As soon as he is with someone else, he feels happy and useful. Yet his life requires him to spend hours alone every day—by "his life" I mean the life he has chosen. He is evidently thus somewhat crazy, just as he says.

New York, 3/30/83

If, as I.C. said the other night, description is an activity in which the writer can begin to resolve the irreconcilability of the written word and the unwritten world, is there a hierarchy of preferences of things to be described? Should one pursue the description of objects that are more and more devoid of salient characteristics, for instance the cigar box given me by the J and R Tobacco Company, a parallelepiped of the barest sort? Or should one aim at portraying objects that are perpetually in flux or, better, that are transformed by our very description of them, like this page? What else could be so transformed? A beautiful woman tattooed with an account of her diminishing beauty—but she wouldn't then be truly something else: simply a woman being treated like a page. Experience itself, past or present: as we represent it in words, it is assuredly modified, it's reduced, it's stripped of what is virtually an infinite ambiguity of interpretation and given only one version of itself—it becomes that other object which is the set of words of our description. Ponge's genius—or part of it—is that he so immediately quits the oyster or cigarette he's describing for other objects to which he metaphorically compares it that the original object and our access to it are left unencumbered by what he has made of it. All his descriptions should carry April Fool's Day as the date of their inspiration.

New York, 4/1/83

Billy was jealous, in a remote way, when he learned from Bobby how Billy's acupuncturist had dealt with him: telling him that he had a lot of depression locked in his body and suggesting after the insertion of the first needle or two that he let it all go, which he did. The reason for the jealousy is that the acupuncturist had never spoken to Billy so directly about his feelings. The reason for the remoteness of the jealousy is that one of Billy's ideas about himself was confirmed by the preferential treatment Bobby got—the idea that he will inevitably be left out; that he will be considered not cruelly or indifferently but without special attention, without the consoling, intimate gesture that means recognition; that he will be condemned to do without the heartwarming knowledge that he belongs to a group, even that of outcasts.

This was not the whole of Billy's reaction. He was pleased that Bobby had experienced so much on his first visit to the acupuncturist, pleased with himself for being the agent of that visit. He told me as well that, after all, it was probably up to him to make his needs clear to the acupuncturist. He was well aware of the grief he was lugging around. . . . Or could it be that in fact it had grown lighter, that it was now so much a part of him that there was no longer either the need or the possibility of separating it from him?

New York, 4/2/83

Maybe my "speech pencil" would be useful for these daily lines: it might put me in touch with the part of me that speech involves. Best pick a topic first rather than let writing-as-I-speak suggest the topic. It might be interesting to see what topics it did bring up; but it would be too much like automatic writing to enable me to start speaking on the page (which isn't "to the page").

Pick a subject, anyway: daffodils. Look, the daffodils are out. The forsythia's out, too, and the sulangeana is opening its buds. "Daffodil" will probably always seem sillier than the flower it names. Because of (a) Daffy Dill and (b) Willie Wordsworth and the gushiness that's stuck to the subjects he wrote about. My own history is involved here. I think I was fussed over (by Capt. Fry? or my mother?) for so loving "I wandered lonely as a cloud," when I was eleven or so. At the time this could only mean yet another distancing from the Real Boys. I'd always excepted the poem from the Wordsworth-I-don't-like, but when I think about it now it sounds typically silly: "lonely as a *cloud*"? "Continuous as the stars that shine" is a haunting verse; but even if the basis of the simile is continuity, to compare wobbly daffodils to invisibly moving stars is like comparing white bunny tails to snowy mountain peaks. So let's do that.

New York, 4/4/83

A week without writing, a week worrying about not writing—Billy Bodega doesn't like it, and yet he wasn't doing much about it while it passed. He said (more to himself than to me) that life will always take first place in his heart—as though writing weren't a part of life, or were somehow a lesser part. Is writing less a part of life than talking on the phone? Than riding in taxicabs? Than taking naps? Billy insists it's not that simple, although he admits he neither understands the situation nor controls it. It is *one* situation—he can admit that, too: the situation of a writer not writing, or not much. He adds that this was a very upsetting week. All the more reason, I told him, to keep the work going and—even better—to confide one's upsets to the virgin page. "Virgin page!" he exclaimed, "that's what I think I'm turning into! It's been like my first times with women, when I was so shocked by the reality of them I couldn't get erect, and desire left me, and I soon decided, life's not so bad without sex. What a joke!" I think what matters is not that he's having that kind of an experience now, but that he's discovered a new way of thinking about the problem. He says he's not up to that. So, I asked, the desire to write left him? "Not true!" The page too lady-like? too womanly? too fucking womanly? "And woman is the page to make one's eternal mark upon? Is that what *you* mean?"

New York, 4/11/83

A man and a woman marry. For their first meal at home she bakes a ham, preparing it as she always does, at the start slicing off both its ends before setting it in the pan. The ham is delicious, her husband delighted. "Why do you make it that way," he later asks her, "slicing the ends off?" "I don't know *why,*" she answers, "except that I learned to do that from my mother." Curious, the husband asks his mother-in-law at their next meeting, "Why do you slice both ends off the ham when you make it in the delicious way you taught your daughter?" "I don't know *why,*" she answers. "I learned how to make it from my mother." The husband insists that he and his wife visit her grandmother, whom he again asks: "You bake ham in a wonderful way that has been adopted by your daughter and then by your granddaughter. Can you tell me why in this recipe one slices off the ends of the ham before cooking it?" "Don't know why *they* do it," the old lady replies, "but when I made it, the ham wouldn't fit in the pan."

This fable, illustrating our inevitable ignorance about why things happen the way they do, was told to us on the first day of the More Time Course, which included many other goodies: how to avoid fatigue by sleeping less, how to manage disagreeable emotions by scheduling them, how to replace paying bills by making contributions to institutions one admires (such as Con Ed, restaurants, taxicabs).

New York, 4/20/83

Billy Bodega says he's feeling good this week. He doesn't understand what happened to him ten days ago. That's not quite true, he immediately adds. "I understand—maybe—why I was in the pits, it's the moving up and on that remains mysterious. The problem is, when you start getting into feeling better—more active, more looking forward to what will happen next, instead of dreading it—you stop checking yourself out. Of course that's a relief, after all those days spent asking what's wrong. But awareness of the introspective sort is blown away by plain enthusiasm. The mechanics of recovery are not observed. They appear to one as no more than a succession of fresh ideas. And the ideas aren't what matter, it's the process of moving that's so powerful."

Billy says that he's realized that committing oneself to work and to working hard and regularly shouldn't be a primary aim. That is something which should and does happen as a by-product of another commitment, one that's both harder and easier to assume: the commitment to high ambition. You have to start from the knowledge that you already are what you're going to become—no, not a corpse, but the master of your life, which means a master of the world, which is nothing more than the page on which your life will be read (is being read). The rest—work, love, health—is just filling in the promising blanks.

Wainscott, 4/23/83

What's the weather going to do? I call to find out: "Showers today, cloudy and cooler tonight." More of the same, and I feel I should mind. Perhaps the steady, conspicuous replacement of blossom by leaf is a welcome lesson that things—indeed, all things—go on happening even when the sky shuts down.

The mockingbird is briefly attractive when he flies: the white of his wings is revealed as he swoops down onto a low wall to catch some minuscule creature, and the wings beat strongly—but he is not beautiful: a bum in a frock coat, albeit a bum with pretensions, or "portensions." Legs astride, head cocked back for sideways glances, pot-bosomed—a comic-opera comedian playing the downfall of William Jennings Bryan. But notice: the tails of the frock coat, no less than the wings, become beautiful in flight, bordered with the same off-white, kite-shaped, full, strong.

Billy tells me that one of his best friends is going through a period of great upset—just as he himself was ten days ago, except that in his friend's case the circumstances themselves are painful (the end of an affair). The symptoms and the disease are the same—terror when confronted by loss, doubt as to one's reality, a sense of terminal failure, chronic ignorance of what one wants in the midst of the fuming acid of change. "Nothing will ever be the same," except oneself, and who wants to rely on that pathetic little monster?

New York, 4/25/83

Billy's friend Bobby told him this morning that, if he could, he should stop drinking. (This is virtually his only non-drinking friend, someone who gave it up years ago.) Bobby allowed that Billy might be fun when he was drunk, but he still hated seeing him drunk because he was so much "less there," and he wanted all of him, or at least as much of him as he could get. Billy was saddened, although not annoyed, by these remarks. He wasn't even sad for long. Admitting that what he'd been told was true, he immediately busied himself with, first, finding reasons for going on drinking and, second, imagining ways to behave when he drank that would short-circuit the change in him that Bobby disliked (or rather repair the short circuits brought about by alcohol and restore a complete grid of presence). I pointed out to Billy that it was hard to react to alcohol with the attentiveness, with the sense of reality that he evidently had in mind. Alcohol was a drug that created impatience, a thirst that got thirstier, and its effects were at least in part physiological, that is to say mechanical. Billy agreed but added that this only made mastery of the problem a more interesting challenge: to achieve it would show that even drunkenness can be an agent of consciousness, that "in vino veritas" need not only refer to involuntary self-disclosure but to possibilities of conscious awareness as well. Billy was serious in telling me this.

New York, 4/27/83

I was introduced to John Keyser at the Knickerbocker Club. He asked me, "Are you Eddie's brother?" "No, his son." My father had certainly looked young at the end of his life, but not "that" young; which could only mean that I looked "that" old—a startling thought. A day or two later I asked my mother to tell me about John Keyser. "He had the *most* beautiful wife. She died tragically—she drove straight into one of those whatever they are that divide the Pulaski Skyway and was killed instantly." She went on to relate an embarrassing encounter with John Keyser. It took place perhaps thirty years after the death of his wife, and my mother had not seen him since then. He was introduced to her. After a moment she asked him, "Was it one of your sons who was married to that beautiful woman who killed herself so tragically?" "It was me," he said.

After being away for months, Billy Bodega went home. His wife was waiting for him with warm, undiminished affection. He wrote me: "I was happy the minute I saw her. The happiness was strangely irrelevant to everything that had happened while I was away, just as what had happened became instantaneously irrelevant to where I now was. It's as though there are parallel continuums in the world, parallel conveyor belts with walls of oblivion rising between them. Effective reality belongs only to the belt we happen to be on at a given moment; the other belts belong to the realm of dreams (memories, anticipations). We are able, of course, to telephone into the past and future, but this is a miracle in which we cannot possibly believe."

Paris, 5/10/83

In spite of his skepticism, Billy Bodega yesterday telephoned into his immediate past. He says it was an experience both comforting and disconcerting. Life, and lives, were going on very well without him, thank you. No, that's not the way it was. There *was* a thank-you, all right, but of another sort. It was as if before leaping off that past track onto his present one, Billy had managed to set in motion some sort of mental support procedures for his friends. He was still, he learned, very much part of their lives. At the same time his absence was accepted wholly. It was as if he had left behind an idea of himself—an undeniably clear idea of himself—as someone committed so thoroughly to his friends that his whereabouts at any given moment didn't matter too much. Billy says that if this is so, he's more than content, even if he hadn't realized what he was accomplishing when he was accomplishing it, even if he still doesn't know *how* he accomplished it. He is more disturbed by the idea that his whereabouts at any given moment don't matter. Is there any point then in being in any particular place at any particular time? Evidently not. The only necessary exception would be the moment of one's birth: it's advisable to be wherever you are right then. Otherwise the idea of you, which is a past-and-future existence, will do very nicely, thank you. Death provides no exception—on the contrary, that's what death is: not being in that particular place at that particular time, and withdrawing into the absoluteness of an idea.

Lans, 5/14/83

My desk is clear, all business done, and my first reaction is to miss the clutter and the chores. But they aren't chores. Most of them are chances to communicate with others, even if only by phone or letter. "Only": that's inaccurate, because being face-to-face with someone usually leads to a consciousness of opportunities missed, of things that couldn't be said; while the further removed the person becomes from that "real" presence (the order being: telephone, letter, thought) the more completely the possibilities are realized.

I think the way to reverse this plainly absurd condition is to have a definite place to go in all one's activities, no matter how mundane. For instance, if I let things happen "naturally," when I see André the two of us will pitch headlong into small talk or into real but irrelevant practicalities that will frustrate my desire to express my appreciation of him. But what if I tell myself: O.K., André's great and you want him to see that you know that, what is it that I truly want of him? What can I ask of him that will involve the two of us in a common aim? It must be this: my house is our house, we're going to make it work together, so what needs to be done to have that happen? "André, *you* tell *me.*"

André was not to be found the last three days, as if to give me the chance to have these ideas. Perhaps this evening I'll find him and try them out. Of course, there will be difficulties. After all, he's insane, and so am I.

Lans, 5/16/83

When I began reading Gregory and Elizabeth Cowan's *Writing* early this morning, I soon found myself overcome by revulsion: not from the book, from myself. Once again, someone knew much more than I did about my own trade. My first reaction was to be suspicious of the book and to find reasons for disqualifying it: it didn't apply to me, it was intended for the graduates of a semi-illiterate school system, its colloquial joviality was redolent with positivism. It was only after I started enjoying the book that I realized that it was myself I had been disqualifying. At some point (quite early on, otherwise I might have begun skimming—"looking at" the book, as M. describes what she does—which can always provide proof of one's prejudices), at some point I saw that the simple "creation" techniques for college essays were potentially useful procedures for imaginative writing. I suddenly found myself among old friends: I'd developed looping for my own courses, I'd used list-making, too, and as for Aristotle's *topoi*—why, there were even scholarly, grandfatherly presences to learn from. I acknowledged that I *was* learning, and that that was my strength and liberty. There's nothing I'm not happy to learn, or relearn, and this excellent book is exactly what I need this very day to begin moving in areas where I'm blocked (such resentments of that condition, such excuse-making!). It's true, as I've told others, that knowing one knows nothing is the best way to be, since life, minute after minute, is never more than being inspired to rediscover what one thought one already knew. I *did* know it, but . . . No, not "but": *and* I'm about to know it again, right now.

Lans, 5/17/83

Last summer's twinge is back, the electric-wire line of pain bisecting my right eye. The circumstances: the weather has changed from cold and bad to cold and good; I'm leaving; I'm leaving M.C. again (although only for three days); I'll be alone in Paris. . . . The thoughts I think are: I'm not well (besides the twinge, I feel generally numb, although I'm hoping a cappuccino and a cigarette from Martine will help that and so prove it's not a symptom of forthcoming flu); and "that's what old age is," an accumulation of little pains (my twinge, my lame hip) and an overall deadening. The cigarette, the coffee, and above all the writing down of these considerations is already lifting the dullness. Now I think: it's all right to blame the weather, a little. The unseasonable cold together with the shift from south wind and rain to north wind and clear skies is, whether physically or psychically, a strong reminder of winter events: one emerges from night curling under a dark refuge of blankets and hanging onto sleep into the fair mountain dazzle that imposes a glory too complete to be believed, winking and blinking. Brightness and cold: a nordic mythical heaven, hard to live up to, to live into; as if we were still sleeping and this was a dream of mindbashing, heartrending intensity, through which we can only grope our way, gulping in the cold air, waiting for some relief—warmth, more clouds and rain. If I have time, after working for an hour and packing and preparing for departure, I should go out into that frosty green world spangled with stiff wildflowers and daffodils lifting their slowly opening heads, and walk or run through it until I know that it's real, and that I in its midst am real, too.

Lans, 5/18/83

Yesterday was a day of chores, and I enjoyed them all (except the first one: I went to the post office, ten minutes away, to retrieve an under-franked letter, only to find that it was no longer there, since such items are only kept five days. I exclaimed complainingly, "Cinq jours seulement!" "Ah, mais ce n'est pas une lettre recommandée," at which I turned away with an unappreciative "Merci" whistled through my teeth, when I could have said a real thank-you for the useful piece of low-grade information I'd learned). After a genial lunch with L. and L., I spent two hours doing four's worth of errands and in doing so was able to speak to Jeannie Edelmann, Robert Bober, Marie-Pierre Galley, Claude Mercier-Ythier, and Tiani Chambard, as well as eleven strangers: the female cashier at La Maison Rustique, where I left an envelope for P.O.L.; a young man and woman at the post office near the Cour de Rohan, who told me the nearest place to find telephone directories; the female cashier at Duriez, who handled my purchase of jiffy bags without an intermediary; two salesmen, one male, one female, downstairs at the PUF bookstore, and two bookcheckers upstairs, who couldn't help me with the book I wanted but who directed me efficiently to Autrement Dit, Marie-Pierre Galley's bookstore; a woman handing out telephone books farther up the Boul' Miche, who provided me unasked with a second set of alphabetic directories and also informed me of the existence of minidirectories (these I chose); and I forgot an earlier meeting with the salesman at Au Cor de Chasse who fitted me for the dinner jacket I'm renting for Glyndebourne; lastly, the African taxi driver who brought me and my bundles home, so courteous he admitted he'd missed a shorter way to go. Isn't this a feast of humanity, a miraculous return on the time and effort invested on one May afternoon in Paris, when spurts of raininess alternated with surges of sun?

Paris, 5/20/83

There's little time today for me to choose what to write about: I'm sitting (I've just sat down) in TGV No. 627 in Gare de Lyon, and the train will leave in two or three minutes. I've had to start my pen moving before the train does.

It's a perfect traveling day, the Saturday of a long weekend (Whitsun or Pentecost), as good, no, better than a Sunday, almost as good as Christmas, New Year's, or Easter. Travelers are few; they have no business to attend to. Most people have already "gotten away."

The train began moving, and rattling since it was still on old tracks, a little too hard for writing. I made notes of things to do, got up to pee, came back. From the seat directly behind mine, another H.M. bounded towards me: Huguette. We hadn't met in ten years. It took me three or four seconds to recognize her—a long time for someone I'd known so well—and what I recognized was not what she looked like but what she was, perhaps in her eyes. . . . She was no longer the adorable doll, no longer the doll grown sadder and plainer, but an interesting, pretty grown-up with a lot of life (work, men, experience) written into her altered head. We grasped each other in spasms of joy, as if wanting on the spot to devour together all the time we had spent apart. And there appeared in us (in her eyes, in the pit of my stomach) an inevitable melancholy as we thought of how much time had passed, while pressing calf against shin and gripping each other's forearm. That melancholy had, in fact, been part of our joy of knowing each other from our first meeting, fifteen years ago. It was our doom—the poignant knowledge that we were not meant ever to live together, that every moment we had could never signify anything beyond its own ecstatic, pathetic self.

Paris—Lyon—Grenoble, 5/21/83

The notion came to me, as I was revising my plans for the next months, for the next years, and potentially for the rest of my life, that each pleasure has its particular use and can serve a purpose. The first example I thought of was opera: its use is enabling me to cry, and my purpose in going to the opera is to let go of thoughts and feelings I would otherwise hold back. There may be more to my operagoing than this, but let's say there isn't: looking at the pleasure it provides in terms of use and purpose can have its own use and purpose. Then mustn't I ask, isn't an opera seat a little expensive for its use? Climbing to the top of a neighboring hill and screaming at the world might work better, and it would certainly be cheaper. Even therapy sessions—for some, a luxury-priced staple—would be cheaper.

At this point other elements of the pleasure of operagoing demand a hearing. I start remembering moments of exaltation without tears—for instance, in Arles one summer, Caballé's rendition of her demanding aria in the second act of *Elisabetta.* She demonstrated a beauty beyond any feeling I was capable of, and it wasn't that of an acrobat, or a prodigious dancer. Perhaps it was like a dancer getting the absolute meaning out of each movement, that meaning being: this is bending forward and nothing else, this is a turn to the right, and nothing else (with an infinite interpretive fallout left to the viewer). Caballé's notes were what singing is, happening to be those of Rossini, and being utterly nothing else but those notes.

So even if there *is* more to opera, evaluating according to use and purpose has a use and purpose.

Lans, 5/23/83

I have a friend who lives a double life, not in the sense that half of it is secret, but that it is divided between two very different places, where he behaves in very different ways. In whichever place he may be, the recollection of the other one fills him with longing; he is thus perpetually made aware of his own imperfection, of his incompleteness.

My friend's work is weaving (and chiefly reweaving) rugs. It's a demanding trade. It requires dexterity, patience, aesthetic judgment, and a willingness to relinquish what is made as soon as it is made. My friend both dreads his work and loves it. It frightens and satisfies him, not the least because of the great attention others pay to it. Or that's what *he* thinks. My own impression is that once people get a rug they look at it for about thirty seconds and as soon as it's on the floor only see it as part of the general aspect of the room it's in; even then, their feet probably notice its presence (or subsequent removal) before their eyes do. But there's no denying that my friend's skills are in demand. He's paid twenty-five dollars an hour, or more, whenever he chooses to exercise them.

Lans, 5/24/83

I may not care about the weather—especially when other things are going well—but just to know that, I have to notice what the weather is: "A lousy day, and I've loved every minute!" One advantage of my new study is that it has no windows and a translucent but not transparent skylight: weather can only be detected as a change in brightness (clouds coming and going) and as a rattle or patter or thrum of rain, hail, or snow. In recent days this has been an especial blessing.

Recent days, in our late May of 1983, have meant bad weather, out of the south as usual, but with the south wind blowing cold, and colder. There were clouds and some rain, then clouds and more rain, and then rain virtually uninterrupted, and finally snow. First, snow at night, next snow into the early daylight hours, today snow at eleven in the morning. This snow doesn't stick and doesn't entirely melt. It leaves an irregular crust over the grass. The grass is very green, as is the sempervivum along the front of the house, which looks positively stiff with pep.

Everything else has been stopped in its tracks. The daffodils across the road have been in bloom for a month. The blossoms of the pear trees, never before so brightly open, are fixed in their expectancy. Tree leaves have stuck their noses out of the twigs—the landscape is a pointillist expanse of green noses. (But the flowers and blossoms will not withstand much more snow. Surely heads can be bowed to the ground and lifted straight only a certain number of times.)

This is weather that makes itself noticed. It's putting my smugness to a fair test.

Lans, 5/25/83

A traveling day: not even ten minutes for writing at home, so these twenty-odd lines must be set down in the stationary moments of travel, while waiting for the train to start moving again. Since Stendhal is the authority for this daily *devoir* (the word means "homework" rather than "duty," and M.C. just used it in that sense: "Alors, tu fais ton devoir?"), it's appropriate that I'm starting it today in the railroad station of the town where he was born. Or is it even faintly appropriate? What can Stendhal have to do with this place (any more than Mozart has to do with Vienna, or Proust with Illiers, where I've sworn I'll never go)? If he does have anything to do with Grenoble, it must be in an act of the imagination, one probably that exercises itself in oppositions— Stendhal expansive and passionate, Grenoble hemmed in and calculating, and so forth. (Not that I haven't come to like Grenoble: Monsieur Dubedout and the Maison de la Culture have opened it, like an oyster. There was light and savor underneath the sealed, calcareous, damp, cutting roughness.) But what city outside Italy, except Paris and New York, could withstand a comparison with Stendhal's spirit and not finish a distant second?

Almost two hours later comes the first chance to complete this day's stint, at Lyon-Brotteaux, where a cold wind is unsurprisingly belying the town's sunny reputation. Later, if train and track are smooth, I can write a page or two of *Cigarettes*. Not doing so would be my one regret of the day.

Grenoble—Lyon, 5/27/83

What is the source of the familiar, panicky disorganization that besets me whenever I come back to Paris (or to New York—but not to Venice: not big enough, or "dangerous" enough)? I don't get up particularly late (between 8 and 9), the errands I have to run are only moderately time-consuming, my priorities are clear to me (writing, studying, perhaps practicing the harpsichord). Nevertheless by 10 or 10:30 my day is enshrouded in a cloud of jittery and also resigned hopelessness: I'm not going to get what I want to get done done. Of course I do get things done, but only the least interesting ones; not that these are useless—they provide a way back into the life of the city, which is life itself. (What I wrote on May 19 describes how nearly exalting this way back can be.) But why should this require giving up my work and most of my "reflective" activity? What are this helplessness and panic about? What are they a fear of, assuming that fear lies behind them? When I was a child, the city streets I knew were places to play in and dream in. They were part of the domain of my reflective life. Did adolescence turn them into places of anxiety—my getting tall, feeling like a conspicuous tall cock, being confronted with instances of love (and thinking: every person I see represents an orgasm) and not seeing how I could ever find sexual solace? Do I now run around doing errands to make the outdoors safe? Why does buying things, especially ones that are relatively expensive, calm me so extraordinarily?

Paris, 5/28/83

This morning M.C. watched a tiny all-brown bird take its first flight, or at least one of its first flights. It had stood on the window of our hotel room, clinging for all it was worth to the rim of the lower sash window. Its mother (more accurately, a much larger bird of the same species—one makes assumptions in such cases) was speaking to it volubly and beating its wings demonstratively as it hovered in the air in front of the smaller bird. I was inevitably reminded of the wren that had nested in the garage at Lans and her swarm of bumblebee-size wrenlets, whom I watched her teach not only to fly but to hunt for food in wall crannies, chattering and indefatigably setting examples throughout her lessons. What is being taught is not only the set of acts that make up the subject of the particular lesson, but another set that will be used by the pupils much later: that of pedagogical method. Isn't it this inconspicuous set of acts that leaves the more lasting imprint? In humans, that is, if not in birds. As soon as we learn how to walk or count or read, it becomes impossible for us to recall the state in which we were ignorant of those talents (even if the difficulties of our learning endure, as is obvious, for instance, from watching the way people walk). What we keep from the learning experience is an idea of how to teach—only an idea, not the true manner in which knowledge was passed on to us. That idea is inevitably charged with our feelings about our teacher, and no doubt with his or her feelings about his or her teacher; so that when it is our turn to teach, we drag in (even physically) a cumulative history of irrelevant psychology. No wonder "culture" is so weighty; no wonder the teaching method I learned from Werner Erhard's courses gave me such an opportunity: I "know," much better than what I learned, the way I learned it, and in this case the associations are "anti-cultural," hilarious, and liberating.

Lewes (Sussex), 6/1/83

Yesterday afternoon N. called, while I was at the Fayollats' watching the Noah-Willander finals at Roland-Garros. She told M.C. that she was too sick to make arrangements for P.'s imminent arrival in New York. I called her back—Bernard said she'd gone outside: could this be true, no matter how clement the weather?—and finally spoke to her around 7 P.M. She spoke in a low, lapsed voice, explaining that the pain of her arthritis was so bad it kept her awake through the night and that she had come down with pneumonia again. She asked me to pray for her, for M.C. ("she has such good vibes") to light a candle, because this was one of the worst crises in her life and she had no desire at this time "to go over to the other side." She cried in a helpless, physical way. Her remarks about praying and lighting candles suggested that her feelings about God were like those about her doctors: she had recently cursed both (God for His injustice, the doctors for their narrowmindedness), and a few days after heaping scorn on her doctor in Berne she had had to call him and ask him to take her into his hospital. She has been behaving angrily with other people as well, she told me. Laurent has been wonderful, keeping her busy with the work that is her one consolation.

At the end of the conversation I told her I loved her, as I had last week when her healer had left her feeling so much better. It was no lie, although I would have a hard time defining the love I feel for her. She has never been motherly to me, or like a mother in my mind. "Mon enfant, ma soeur?" Except that she's ninety-nine times as tough and experienced as I am. We were married on a 6th of June.

Lans, 6/6/83

And Niki's pain is less, she probably doesn't have pneumonia, she's certainly not dying; and we reserved a Lancia to drive from Grenoble to Venice later in the month; and David K. is happily settled in Palazzo Barbaro, and all his witty sweetness could be heard over the telephone; and the sky is of a blue that makes you look into it for drifts of angelic gold, the air clear but not perfectly clear because there is that faintest, lightest moisture in it, making it so delectable to look through (and almost *at*) that you want to rub your skin with it—air just thick enough to make spaces palpable: on such a morning, nothing feels wrong. Not calls that don't go through, or phones not answering or being answered by people who switch you to the wrong extension or say silly, time-wasting things. Time can't be wasted on a June morning like this. "Weather does not matter," but it has its uses. Weather like this is for letting go of resistances to pleasure and for stocking up on the love of created things. Perhaps if the redstarts nesting in this study shat directly onto my pate I might be discouraged in my enthusiasm in (not "for") the animal and vegetable worlds. Otherwise it seems likely that the pleasure bestowed today on all five senses will open body and being to intensities of appreciation for which neoplatonic interpretations sound at best impressionistic. This is weather for playing God yourself.

Lans, 6/7/83

These last days have been productive ones. I've done the work I wanted (i.e. I've kept the several projects I'm concerned about moving) and paid attention as well to mundane activities. There are two flaws in my life thus organized. First, I've not set foot outside our place—M.C. has had to do all the public chores. This is not only an unfair situation but a false one: barricaded withdrawal is not the natural state of a social animal. Second, even though I haven't had a drop even of wine in half a week, an insomniac pattern is installing itself in the rhythm of my days. I wake up around dawn (5 A.M.) and lie awake for an hour and a half, then sleep until a quarter of nine. My first awakening comes at the end of a dream, not necessarily a frightening or disagreeable one; I lie in bed in a not-violent anxiety that generally gives way to "thinking"; I seem unable to get back to sleep before M.C. gets up for E.'s departure to the lycée, at which time I work up a broth of sexual fantasies and in its midst (and among the pleasant disintegration of images that runs before sleep) begin dozing, dreaming many little light dreams.

The insomnia is a nuisance in that it takes two hours out of my working time. Getting up late does not make me unhappy or ill at ease with myself (only embarrassed with others), but the form it takes points to a double resistance on my part: to the unconscious experiences that make themselves present in my night sleep, and to the prospect of the new day. And what else is there in my life? It's as though I were refusing to accept my acceptance of the world (*my* world). I must ask Billy Bodega what he thinks about this.

Lans, 6/8/83

Productivity always falls on its ass when I arrive in Paris. Sometimes there are excuses: things must be done before a certain day or hour (getting cash before the bank closes on Friday afternoon). Today, however, I finished my errands by 1 P.M. It's now 5:30, and I'm only starting to write. There's still time to write a lot, of course, and I will. This will at least be a step up, from doing nothing to doing what might be called an unacceptable minimum. The scenario—I once wrote a line of poetry about it, something like: "The day is lost, and possibilities come out of hiding"—my scenario is to wait until it's too late, so that no matter what gets done will be disappointingly small. Since the need for self-denigration is sure to be satisfied, the doing no longer matters—the weight is taken from the task, and the task is then easily done. That is what is happening today.

Why I haven't succeeded in turning the habits of days in the city around as I did those in the country (a little—not *right* around, as the expression suggests) is more a question than a real problem. That is, the matter may simply concern scheduling—of imagining a less obvious, more fragmented, more exciting way of expressing the desire to work without giving up the valuable human dousing my hectic visits here provide. But watch out: "fragmented, exciting" mustn't become an excuse for getting *less* done.

Paris, 6/11/83

In the course of the e s t training you build a "center" for yourself. Following the specifications of the trainer, you not only imagine it but go through the motions of fashioning it, standing up, stepping in one direction then another, modeling the various parts with your hands according to the image forming behind your closed eyes. Last winter, when I transformed Niki's old studio into my new study, I noticed when I was through how very similar it was to the imaginary center I'd concocted seven and a half years earlier. Obvious similarities: bare stone walls, suffused light, spaciousness, an array of bookshelves to my right. Of course the differences are many: aside from the bookcases, there are none of the magical knowledge-apparatuses of the center, and even the bookcases look different (although their function is perhaps less different than one would expect), and in my reality the stone walls are discontinuous and rise only as far as the peaked roof allows them— in the center, they rose at least eighteen feet, in truth they rose as high as I wanted them to go; the roof was flat.

It was only yesterday, on the train bringing me home, that I realized what the greatest similarity of all was: neither my study nor my center has any windows. One might say that this is what makes the place (do I mean both places?) my *center* and *my* center. For all its roominess the world here is self-enclosed. I have to leave it when a car arrives and I want to know whose car it is. Light comes straight down from the sky. The horizon is filled with human artifacts of my choosing: the outside world has been brought inside for my knowledge, use, and pleasure. The place is safe and rich with all the potentiality I need to invent, remember, and love the everything-else that lies beyond these massive, opaque walls.

Lans, 6/15/83

Once my "Armenian" poems are finished, I would like to start keeping a poetic journal, writing a (proto-)poem each day to record some appropriate event—a shift in thought, feeling, perception, the gain or loss of an experience of life. Reading Empson's essay on the Byzantium poems gave me the idea, or encouraged it. The first versions of the poems are so far from the clangorous resoluteness of the final ones, are so close to the meanderings of private thought (by meanderings I suppose I mean the writing down directly of feelings one *wishes* to produce) that it occurred to me I needn't be so severe either with myself or my material when I write a poem. In a way I've never been severe— poetry for me has always been an occasion for play, for chucking words around to see what happens, for trying out methods of arranging words. The severity has applied to what is going on with me (within me, without me . . .) at the time. I write poetry in a kind of relief, but I don't let the relief extend to what in my mind and bones might need relieving. Except when I do: "Shrub Air" was an instance. And in that poem and in a few others there is an original grain. I don't really understand it. (Of course, there is no question of getting real relief from writing a poem— or even a letter.) So why not return to that manner (not that style, but the way the poem was composed), why not use poetry to say what can't otherwise be said, just as it's meant to do? If nothing else, it would keep me in touch with the stuff of individual words, and provide daily material for many Byzantiums.

Lans, 6/16/83

A sure way of appreciating one's house is to keep leaving it. With only four days to spend in mine between a weekend in Burgundy and over seven weeks in Italy and America, this lumpy and demanding farm-house on a small mountain in a cold part of a not particularly interesting French province has a heartrending appeal for me. The chores that need doing and that I shall not have the time to do seem like opportunities for self-realization that cannot possibly be found elsewhere. And this is true enough. There will be other opportunities, but not of the same kind. What happens here is a unique fusion of the unending drama running inside my head with material objects outside me. These objects—not only furniture and paintings and books and a piano but plants and trees and stones—were in many cases chosen by me to be where they are as a function (usually unconscious) of that inner phantasmal drama; and when they weren't chosen, when I found them where they were, their existence and situation determined by others or by natural processes, twenty-five years of staring at them have made them not mine (ownership of land and landscape is a fiction) but me. The ash tree looming between the two houses, the right-angle bend in the little stair, the seepage of light and sweet dawn air through the gap left by the flatly hung Indian cloth over my bedroom window, are more what I am, certainly, than the hair growing on my chest, or the tune in my head, or the ideas in my head in fact—including these ideas about the central place filled in my being by these walls, these bordered fields, this golden-clouded sky.

Lans, 6/20/83

Mathews, Matthews, Mathew, Matthew, Matthïesson, Matthiae, Matthias, Matthisson, Mattei, Matteotti, Mathias, Mateus, Matthieu, Mahieu, Madeu, Mathet, Mathie, Mathiez, Matisse, Matthis, Matteo, Mathelin, Mathiret, Mathiot, Mathon, Matou, Méhu, Matthaeus, Μαθθαιος, Ματθαιος—"probably a shortened form of the Hebrew equivalent to Theodorus," i.e. gift of God—"gift of Yahweh." Apostle, evangelist. According to Eusebius he wrote "only at the spur of necessity": "when about to go also to others, [he] committed to writing in his native tongue the Gospel that bears his name; and so by his writing supplied, for those whom he was leaving, the loss of his presence." According to legend, his later labors took place in the Parthian kingdom, where he died "a natural death at Hierapolis (=Mabog on the Euphrates)." "In Christian art (following Jerome) the Evangelist Matthew is generally symbolized by the 'man' in the imagery of Ezek. i.10, Rev.iv.7"—i.e.: "Their faces were like this: all four had the face of a man and the face of a lion on the right, on the left the face of an ox and the face of an eagle"; and: "[In the centre, round the throne itself, were four living creatures, covered with eyes, in front and behind.] The first creature was like a lion, the second like an ox, the third had a human face, the fourth was like an eagle in flight." Brewer: St. Matthew is "represented in art (1) as an evangelist—an old man with long beard—an angel generally standing behind him dictating his gospel; (2) as an apostle, in which capacity he bears a purse, in reference to his calling as a publican [he was thought to be a tax-gatherer or a customs official]; sometimes he carries a spear, some-times a carpenter's rule or square. His symbol is an angel, or a man's face, and he is commemorated on Sept. 21st." (Elsewhere: "with a pen in his hand, and a scroll before him, looking over his left shoulder at an angel." Yet elsewhere: "With a halberd, with which Nadabar killed him [in Ethiopia?], or with the Gospel, and a purse or a money-box. . . . His most ancient symbol is a man's face.")

What we know about St. Matthew ("know" may not be the right word) produces an impression that is sympathetic rather than forceful. Unlike the other evangelists and the Biblical figures with whom they are identified, he does not benefit from the symbolic presence of an animal—a presence that confers on the other three an aura of strength and of being at home in the order of nature. At first glance, what

Matthew does have—an angel—might lead us to think that he was privileged, that he belonged to the divine order; but his attitude, "with a pen in his hand and a scroll before him, looking over his left shoulder," sets us right. The place of the animal has been given to the angel out of need: for whatever reason, St. Matthew cannot manage to set down his gospel without dictation. He cannot find inspiration within himself. He feels he is not a writer—he writes "only at the spur of necessity." Perhaps this spur and a lack of time contribute to his difficulty. On the other hand, his willingness to write so as "to supply his loss" is a winning trait, although one can wonder if Matthew sensed that by resorting to the written word he was not replacing his presence, only replacing his absence with yet another absence, one even more subject to misinterpretation than the void his departure would leave behind. Matthew probably thought: "If I were staying here, I would say certain things"; and the things he would have said are the things he wrote down. And those things were read, and reread, and they became a text to be deciphered and interpreted, without his voice, his gestures, or his faculty of response to restore whatever meaning he had first intended.

And then St. Matthew's other symbol is the face of a man—poor thing. I'm glad he's my patronym.

Additional note: in the quotation from Revelations, he appears third; as I remember, three was "my" number when I was little.

Lans, 6/22/83

At last, after many years of not (really) trying, I began to know Ruth. Previously I had spoken with her the time it took a taxi to go from Greenwich Village to Sixty-somethingth Street. I've now spent several hours with her, most of them in the company of others, it's true, but who is to say that less communication takes place between two people in such circumstances? On my first night here, after a day that had been long, exciting, happy, and demanding, we spoke together for around an hour, towards midnight. The next day we had drinks before dinner and then dinner, *à cinq*. Today I was one of three to accompany her to the station; she was going to Milan for a day before returning to America.

I had remembered her as being lively and funny. She seems, rather, bright, nice, and serious, almost earnest. We talked a lot about teaching. She dislikes the policy of her college towards women—it amounts, she feels, to encouraging them to learn how to prove they are competent in an unchanging masculine world. At our group dinner as well as at other times, she expressed enthusiasms for Rome and Venice that seemed strangely—perhaps hypocritically?—simple: Rome was an eater's paradise, Venice a pedestrian's charming labyrinth. Was she wittier and profounder before? D.K. told me about an uneasy affair to which she had referred (her Milanese friends are the brother and sister-in-law of her former lover). She had fallen in love with a colleague whose wife was dying; the affair had begun before she died. Afterwards, many of her friends worried that she would see the man through his mourning and that he would then find someone else and leave her. This is exactly what happened. His remarriage last January, with a woman who was virtually Ruth's replacement, revived the old pain. She is now attractive but not as attractive as she should be. It is as though she wore her self-sufficiency too overtly: a little too heavy, and not made up and coiffed well enough.

I liked her very much. I wanted her to know that she was a woman who should love and be loved. (I made a point of telling her what wonderful legs she has.) At the station, when she appeared in the window of the new railway car, I offered to take a picture of her with her camera, but she said no, decisively. So I held on to her image. She was leaning part way through the lowered window, whose polished bronze rounded rectangle provided her with a luminous gold frame, the many bolts that fastened it forming with their cross-shaped indentations a border of stylized stars that set her appropriately off as a Tiepolesque, sexy-sweet Madonna, smiling calmly as she abandoned the three of us to our little-boy lives.

Venice, 6/26/83

20 During the days—at least fourteen of them—when I might have added to these

19 pages and didn't (I was using translation once again as a warm-up to start my day's

18 writing), so many possible subjects occurred to me and were let go with regret. And

17 letting them go meant just that—I can't remember a single one of them (although no

16 doubt I know methods of recovering them). But there isn't any loss, because such

15 subjects are the merest pretexts: they don't ever add anything to what gets written,

14 and probably they are no better than other—no matter what other —points of departure.

13 Lovely ideas belong to amateurs, or, worse, to might-have-been writers. Lost possibilities

12 mean none at all. Nothing better than writing makes grotesquely obvious the obvious

11 truth that what is is; or (to put it another way) the Marxist truth that

10 there is no value outside of work done. This does not, however, exclude the

9 "unfinished masterpiece": once it is written down, a project or idea, no

8 matter how incomplete, is real work. (See Barthes on this topic.)

7 Certainly everything I've ever written seems to me to constitute a series of

6 holding actions against the day when I can mount my triumphant

5 "major" assault on the towers of fame. And so, probably, will seem all the things

4 I shall write in the future; because either that certainty

3 that one will achieve a moment of greatness never comes, or, when

2 it comes, I won't even know it; or perhaps, more sadly, I shall

1 notice but no one else will—and what's the point of being "great" all alone?

Wainscott, 7/16/83

Anxiety about writing feels like: I am poor in words, ideas, and feelings, and when I sit down to write, this poverty will be revealed. It is another example of the general rule about fear: fear has nothing to do with its object. (When I jump off a thirty-foot ledge into the sea, my experience bears no resemblance to what I so paralyzingly apprehended before making the jump.) It's obvious to me that if I have a problem with words, ideas, or feelings, it will be due to their excess, not their lack. I'm stuffed from head to toe with them, and my reluctance to sit down at my desk, which this morning has led to my writing a letter, making several phone calls, and preparing a pot of lamb stock, all of which could have been done another day or even another week, must be regarded as definitely insane. Knowing what I do—how much I enjoy writing, how many ways there are to put the resources of language into action—I feel worse than insane (insanity still has a certain romantic attraction): I feel stupid. I think that what I must do to make the stupidity manageable is to apply to it a method that has worked with even more painful conditions: I shall schedule it. Every morning—*early* every morning— I'll set aside ten minutes and concentrate exclusively on feeling anxious about sitting down to write. The most rudimentary sense of absurdity should get me going by minute number three.

Wainscott, 7/19/83

We say: to write about a subject, to write on a subject, to write of something; also to write for and against something or someone; also to write by a certain light, and with the implement of our choice, and to our correspondents. About, on, of, for, against, by, with, to: is there a logic in this set of prepositions, or a logic in the set of missing ones, like around, in, into, at, inside, outside? Would it be possible, and if so what would it be like, to write around, or in, or into—to write around politics, write in compost preparation, write into love, write at fiction, write inside the genesis of the universe, write outside a friend? (Is there yet another logic or consistency in the set of prepositions that I haven't been able to think of at this moment?) Writing around a subject or a person seems a promising possibility. The subject or addressee would play a role like the letter *e* in *La Disparition*—never appearing and at the same time figuring as an object of unrelenting attention, staring us in the face all the harder for never being named. Writing in might require participation in the subject at the moment of writing—in the case of compost preparation, here I am knee-deep in mulch. (*All* writing would be an act of writing in writing.) Writing into: discovery, aggressive curiosity. Writing at: against, or towards, or in haphazard approach. And writing inside—inside the genesis of the universe: where else can one be? It's all so easy then. (Forget belief.) And writing outside: out of a context larger than the subject, so that we can at last see it whole, as if we had only five minutes left to live, or five seconds.

Wainscott, 7/21/83

Two days ago, after visiting J.A., I noticed that for the first time I can remember I hadn't been depressed by being inside a hospital. There was no reason not to be depressed—J.'s floor provided the customary glimpses of bedridden patients not only very sick but very old, attended by relatives only slightly less old; of friends and other relatives waiting to see a patient or a doctor, worn by anxiety and expectancy; of innumerable bustling nurses, nurse's assistants, doctors, cleaning women, male attendants (one of whom took J. down for his test), all concentrating on their work and unwilling (no doubt rightly) to attend to the weight of sadness, fear, and discouragement that visitors and patients bear. Why wasn't I as usual struck with that stupefied numbness, containing a strong penchant for going to sleep? It's true that J. wasn't visibly sick; but his hospital pajamas (neo-Cacharel), urinals, and I.V. attachment proffered a sufficient image of sickness to hypnotize me. It was, furthermore, a nice summer day, hot outside, a little cooler in the ward—a perfect reminder of the Siena hospital after P.'s first convulsion. But I accepted being where I was and didn't try to distract myself with reminders of what I would be doing later on. Can I actually have grown used to hospitals or, worse, can I find being in them a "natural" situation? Perhaps the change comes from realizing that they are not only necessary but can actually work. After the deaths of Loulou, and Bob, and my father, and G.P., N. was helped, J.A.'s life was saved last year, and now he has been promptly cured without any but the most unavoidable discomfort. Still, I plan to stay away from them, except as a happier visitor.

Wainscott, 7/22/83

I'm tempted to do twenty lines of automatic writing. It's fast and fun (or "carefree" at least) and sounds like a good way to loosen up at the start of the day. (This writing day is starting at 11 A.M. . . .) But I won't. No matter how mannered these stints may be (any mode repeated enough agglutinates rhythms and sentence patterns so that it tends to lapse into a settled way of thinking), automatic writing is almost always more so. The first sentence scribbled down suggests a mode that is maintained to the very end. The result is too smooth, too homogeneous. Still, facility alone doesn't explain the temptation. I might say things that I'm not saying here, let subjects emerge, even indirectly, to which I don't give myself access. In these workouts I don't feel free to write only for myself; I'm checked by the subliminal thought that some day I may type up these daily ruminations to see if they "add up to something." So others may eventually see them, now, or even after I'm dead, and writing down certain things could upset and retroactively modify relationships that I now depend on—M.C., my children, my friends. Perhaps I should have here written fictions or a fiction. I could have expressed my concerns forthwith, but the invented framework of situations would be strong enough to short-circuit any autobiographical reading of my words. That would have meant a very different approach from what I've manifested here. Perhaps it will be possible later on. For now I'll stick to what I've been doing, long enough to have the pleasure of amassing enough material to show that I can, by following Stendhal's advice, write what in bulk if not in form amounts to a book.

Wainscott, 7/23/83

There may be selfishness and laziness in my wanting to stop writing about G.P.'s work and perhaps to refuse ever to undertake a translation of *La Vie mode d'emploi,* but I also have a more passionate motive. I liked and admired (and like and admire) G.'s work, but it was G. I loved. In the assumption that I should look after his books now that he's dead (M.B.: "Il est incroyable que tu ne sois pas à Cérisy") lies another assumption: that his books, being "all that is left of him," are in fact a part of him. This assumption strikes me as being not only false but repellent. My love for G. had absolutely nothing, *nothing* to do with his writings. I had never read a word by him when we met. My interest in his work flowed from our friendship, never the reverse. Often I felt that reading his work constituted a kind of inevitable chore, one I willingly did because of my feelings for him. It's true that I didn't pay proper attention to *Les Revenentes* or *Espèces d'espace* on their appearance, but with the possible exceptions of *La Clôture* and *La Vie . . .* and the unquestionable exception of *W,* what he wrote seemed almost a distraction from what was taking place between us, and was at best something that provided us with material to talk about. (He was, on the other hand, marvelously attentive to my projects—but they were projects, that is, ideas. He couldn't fairly judge the quality of their realization, which thus remained irrelevant, until he had translated them.) Why should I now busy myself with these remains? Translating G. or writing about him continually upsets me with reminders of my friend now lost forever to me; reminds me, too, how pleased we both would have been if I were doing such work with him alive, and how "useless" it is now. To pretend otherwise is a bestial piety.

Wainscott, 7/25/83

Learn how to watch your feelings and let them come and go—that was the advice D.P. had learned (from reading Krishna Murti, I think) and told us had been useful to him. It resembles a sometime instruction *I* know, "Just notice your thoughts (or feelings or sensations) and let them be"; and of course it is useful, although in the scuffle of battle, such as a conversation, it's always seemed more a wishful than an attainable goal. Perhaps it is part of the mastery of martial artists and of conversationalists like Chesterton. To watch myself is in any case a lovely prospect: to become a landscape animated with birds large and small, coming and going according to the hours of the psychic day and the seasons of the moral year, is certainly a relief after the struggle to be this and do that while I'm actually being that and doing this. My thoughts, my feelings can then simply go on leading their inevitable lives, and I don't have to worry whether they're beautiful or ugly or happy or frightening or (above all) real or false. And after watching the crows of remorse shattering the silence of early day and the grosbeaks rustling in the undergrowth of what-will-I-do-next and the heron perched at the pond's edge to give the place a serious Taoist air, I can at last enter the landscape myself and start going about my business, surrounded by my peaceful or agitated ideas and emotions, walking across the lawns of memory and through the groves of knowledge (oak and pine: inspiration and labor), feeling more at home in the world that surrounds me now that I've finally realized that all of it (even you, Henry Kissinger) is right inside my head.

Wainscott, 7/26/83

Writing well is so hard—that's why it's fun to go for. Did Roland
Barthes have the trouble I do in persuading his prose to reflect or
incorporate his "body"—what we would once have called his nature?
(The writing seems at once so personal and so natural.) He probably
did. Most of us will go to great lengths to avoid looking at our "body,"
or to conceal it once we admit that it's there (that it's us). Those efforts
at avoidance and concealment are what we first set down on the page;
what, more exactly, we wrap our bodily meanings in. Naturalness of
style is not this spontaneity, the spontaneity is all wrappings, which
have to be peeled away before naturalness can be achieved. (But
"peeling" is too gentle a word. One has sooner or later to introduce
metaphors of scissors, knives, pruning hooks, blasting materials.) With
every book I write I hope to have discovered procedures that will take
care of the clutter before the first sentence is written, so that I can
"simply" write what has to be written. There is no way out of the
writing process, even when using a minute vocabulary as in "Their
Words, For You" or eliminating words containing the letter *e*. . . . It is
in the *process* of unwrapping that I become present, for all to see. (*The
Conversions* felt different. The writing was inspired by a tone so strong
as to be taken on the way one takes on a role: writing was something I
could *act.*)

(Above I wrote: "incorporate his 'body.' " "Incorporate" can hardly
be right. What does happen? Transcorporation? Writing is the translation of one body into another.)

Wainscott, 7/29/83

What makes it possible for me to live a city life in the country is the telephone. Just as in New York or Paris, I sit at my desk for at least an hour every day (much longer when J.A. was in the hospital) talking to friends and doing business. Everything that happens happens inside the blind aural world that is altogether independent of surroundings. (Where would this not be so? In prison? Under bombardment? On one's deathbed? Probably not.) It is a tremendous convenience, I mean to one's need to escape from where one is (read: my need to escape from where I am), in time as well as space: as I busy myself in the telephonic universe, the day slips by. Without the telephone, what would I do? I would be forced to turn to distractions in the time and space around me. Errands to be run, chores to do outside, pleasures of the waters and woods that are right at hand (I think of my constantly deferred promise to myself to sit with binoculars behind the woodshed and detail the extraordinary bird life taking place in the oaks, pines, and shrubbery that begin a few yards farther on). Whatever way out I chose, it would be an active one; and activity of course restores energy and focus. The harder I worked at this kind of distraction, the more inevitably and frequently I would be brought back to my desk and the work waiting to be done, work so dear to my happiness and so inimical to the dis-satisfaction which I apparently must always create before allowing happiness to emerge (if at all).

Wainscott, 7/30/83

Fog moves in at evening, spends the night, and hangs around in the morning: visually, November; to the touch, a hammam; overall, sluggish gloom. Will it be burned or blown away? Not likely. The sun is too distant, the wind brings in more fog when it moves the rest along. But there comes a noticeable later-than-daybreak brightening. It happens slowly; but little by little you realize that this is the slowness of irresistible change. You start enjoying the Creation-like effect—the Creation according to Joseph Haydn.

Seeing G.H. yesterday was shocking. He was hidden inside a new body and head. I wasn't sure who he was (and it was only a year ago that I last saw him). He came up to say hello, and we talked a while. He's funnier than ever. He left me with a strong reminder of my wish to write about him at length, treating his oeuvre as such, doing him justice, retrieving the genius from the incrustations of accident, time, and irrelevant gossip so that it would shine unmistakably forth. Behind this wish lay another: if I accomplished my task, his prime body would emerge from the overlays now hiding it, and I could recognize and love him as he was when I met him twenty-one years ago.

A new manifestation of the urgency with which bad news is transmitted: Bobby's father called England to announce Francis Plimpton's death. I've done as much. We must then feel, more or less: he was so clever, so eminent, and look, he's dead, and we're still here.

Wainscott, 8/1/83

Stendhal meant something different from this. He meant, not writing about anything, but adding twenty lines to a work under way. Then his rule guaranteed high productivity (at least at first-draft level): 20 lines x 300 days = 6,000 lines—about 200 pages, or the better part of one of my novels, if not of his. Did he follow the rule? If he did, did it prepare him in some way for the incredible fifty-two day binge on which he dictated *La Chartreuse?* (Why does dictation, practiced by two novelists perhaps my favorites, so frighten me? Go ahead, see what happens. Your Walkman won't tell.) Does writing every day foster a style that is one's own—that is, a way of writing uniquely artificial and at the same time "natural," like G.P.'s unhurried sentences and Stendhal's own hurrying ones? Maybe. I'm skeptical, because I remember starting to write a novel "spontaneously" on my typewriter and finding that what came out was, syntactically, late Henry James (that other dictator). I also feel that behind these daily warm-ups there is another or several other writers whom I'm imitating unawares, especially as I approach the zone of the page where the twentieth line is coming to an end, and that an end is more than a cessation, more too than a conclusion (conclusions being unacceptable to those who practice modernism), the expression of a wry awareness that although you and I feel and speak, any speaking of our feelings will be imperfect, fragmentary, and expressive only through its very failure to express.

Wainscott, 8/2/83

Stephanie L., who answered the phone when I called this morning ("You mean you haven't heard the news? You're calling out of the blue?") had a son, Joseph, on July 24, over a month before his normal time of birth. He was doing well—"breathing room air" (not that of the isolette, as it's now called) and "drinking my milk" (meaning he was "off the I.V."). The lovely sweetness of Steffie's voice was not enough to still my anxiety or my memories. A four- or five-pound creature with a needle in its arm, four to six weeks in the hospital. . . . Well, Steffie will make it up to him. I told her (and David too: he was on the other phone) about P. and wished I hadn't: what they wanted was reassurance. So I said nothing about his galaxy of diseases or his convulsions and comas and mentioned only his late-developing eyesight as a possible consequence of premature birth. As for the rest, I asserted that P. had soon after his birth come into normal health. And who knows what the connections have been between his problems and his shortened stay in N.'s womb. The stay itself was already problematical. Was it there, as I've imagined, that he began believing that his survival among us depended on precariousness, danger, suffering? When he was born early on that blue Majorca morning, the feast of Santiago and San Felipe, he was in spite of his skinned-rabbit leanness so perfect, so apt for life, inspiring love and laughter even in those first days, surviving a cold and an intestinal infection and the affectionate neglect of the nurses. Some day he must see himself as that perfection and forget thoughts of blame and pity, becoming that first self once again.

Wainscott, 8/5/83

The end of our visit is approaching, and with it the temptation to discount the time remaining. The feeling goes something like: I did what I did, and it's too late to catch up with what I didn't do. This is not only not true, it's the worst advice to give yourself. The way to make departures and other kinds of endings smooth and (who knows?) enjoyable is not to leave yourself more time than you need so as to get everything organized in advance, but to go on living as busily as you can and do everything efficiently and quickly by leaving yourself slightly *less* time than you comfortably need. But here there is an important qualification: "living busily" does not mean doing this or that or any old thing—that is only procrastination disguised, it only heightens the inevitable anxiety leavetaking inspires. Living busily must mean going on doing what most matters to you, and even more so—work, love, awareness. It is probably enough just to notice how all your manners of functioning still continue, and that their rising intensity (due to the pressure of anxiety) may be what is making you pretend that in these circumstances they don't matter. All those ideas and sensations and feelings pushing through us—and we look out the window at the grave-yards passing, or fall asleep, or have another precautionary pee. I know that we're all insane at ordinary times, but now it seems more than ordinarily foolish not to savor the apple as we bite into it—an apple from a tree you planted in your own childhood backyard.

Wainscott, 8/6/83

I had planned today to write to myself about the phrase "in a manner of speaking." The plan was to explore the way it was used—I hadn't much to say about it right off, except that it probably covers more than the multitude of small sins for which it serves as a small excuse. (This reminds me of a note I made once to use in dialogue—"Suntan covers a multitude of sins"—and suggests the question: what is the written equivalent of cosmetics?) Since jotting down the phrase, I've had several intense experiences of the ocean, the ocean as it is known to a swimmer setting off from a beach, and I can hardly write about anything else. Here is an earlier jotting about that, too: "feeling the sand sucked from under my feet through my toes by the receding wave in which I'm standing." A pleasure like a vibrator intermittently but regularly applied: I noticed it yesterday at some point during my midday swim, which I can't otherwise much remember. I remember better, although still not very well, since I'd had a lot of wine, driving to the beach for an after-midnight swim: swimming naked, off an empty beach (but a car was parked close to its access point), the waves small enough to cradle, to not hide, our phosphorescent swirls. Then this morning, around eight, entering sullen unclear water heaving oilily under the fog of early day: no magic left from last night, the beach in that light looking weary and littered (bright sun whitens the litter out). Finally, after leading Léo into the reasonable surf, swimming out on my noon exercise stint: stung in the face once but seeing nothing in the water, then seeing on the surface, with my head above water, a jellyfish one foot away without realizing that I'd been stung again, then ducking underneath the surface and starting to swim my way through a school of jellyfish—I started to say hundreds of them, but I saw (let's settle for this) "many," I didn't want to take time to count or even avoid them, I wanted to be away from them, even though their sting is no worse than that of nettles. It was the panic fear of an idea that had me squirming to get past and stay past them until I was close to the beach, where Léo was flirting with the waves. And just what was that idea?

Wainscott, 8/8/83

The idea, of course, was that of being trapped; or more exactly *caught.* There was punishment involved, if only of having been so stupid as to be there in that school of jellyfish, when I could have stayed on the beach or at least on the beach side of it. I thought while still surrounded of a perhaps not evident question: are they male or female? The answer —it may have provoked the question—was evidence itself: no one could conceive of a jellyfish being male. Soft, diaphanous, languid—so many red-blond longhaired heads, of girls or young women, hovering in cloudy submarine space. Feminine too (I know what I'm talking about is my own irrational vision of women, or "Woman," not women themselves) in the non-aggressive punishment they inflict. We can go unscathed if we do not approach them; but we do approach, and molest with our desire, and are stung—the Lulu effect. And: "it isn't fair"; "I didn't know"; "I wish I'd never gotten involved." The ordinary French word for jellyfish is *méduse* (as far as I know, in English medusa is a zoological term): the allusion is not to the gorgon's petrifying face but to her "snaky locks." ("The tangles of Naëra's hair," the snare of poor males.) These jellyfish suggested not only hair but silk—the silk of nightgowns and negligees—memories of my mother having breakfast in bed, or dressed up for an evening party, long, long ago. But of course one medusa would have been enough for that. Their being so many was a recreation of some suppressed fantasy of dread—being hopelessly outnumbered,* and, worst of all, outnumbered by a certain multiplication of my desire: the longing for one woman after another so that I could be enveloped by consoling femininity as in the time when all women were One. That multiplication was now turned against me, as I knew it must be, as I knew it should be, bringing a deserved chastisement proportional to my unholy wish.

New York, 8/11/83

*What I involuntarily wrote was: "being hopelessly numbered . . ."

I just spent half an hour cataloguing a few more of my mother's books. It's slower work than I remembered. The task I first set myself was to get through a shelf, but one look told me that was too much; then three of a shelf's five squares; and I've had to settle for two. Today, as I was bringing down the books from the second square, having left the other half on the platform of the stepladder in an intermediary move, the ladder collapsed, pitching the pile of books onto the strip of stone floor between bookcases and rug. The bindings or boards of several books were fractured. I was particularly sorry that this had happened to Klingerer's *Animals in Art and Thought,* a book which my father had often consulted, and which was still marked with a great number of little slips of torn paper. My father had probably done the marking while he was assembling materials for his own projected book on animals in art. It was one of the projects he undertook after he had "retired." (The quotation marks have a meaning the opposite of their usual one: he was retired for all practical purposes, but he denied it for years, perhaps till the end of his life.) The project never got very far; my father is dead; the book is broken—I was sucked down into the melancholy sentiment that nothing lasts, that everything is present so transiently and fragilely that there is no point in holding on to anything long enough to take proper care of it. This is true, in a way, the crux being: what do we think the "point" is? "Essayer méticuleusement de retenir quelque chose, de faire survivre quelque chose." This is enough, and all—at least in *that* domain.

New York, 8/12/83

I've missed you, opening pages of my writing day. What I missed particularly was the inevitable and bearable crunch of my theoretical "willingness to write" with the touching of penpoint to paper. It's a good warm-up exercise I've given myself: there's no conceivable reason not to write twenty lines about anything or something, and twenty lines are enough (would ten or five be equally so?) to banish the hesitancy that breeds telephone calls and household chores and prolongs the reading of newspapers, L.L. Bean catalogues, and articles in *Raritan*.

It's now time to start writing these lines again every working day. I shall remember to refuse to think, Is what I'm writing good or bad, interesting or not? (Is anything uninteresting?) Are there other explicit or implicit rules I've made for myself? Certainly. I am to avoid automatic writing—it has other uses. I am not to avoid "qualities" of writing any more than I am to worry about them. Many 20-liners are about the events of my life, but this indicates a habit, not a rule; perhaps I should vary my topics systematically. That doesn't matter. What matters is to address, unhurriedly and without procrastination, the page that, because it is the first of many to be faced during the day, is the most discouraging and the most liberating. After it, nothing but the happiness of writing awaits me.

New York, the day of the dead, 1983

With certain friends comes a euphoria that dissolves my doubts and reticences, so that I "give myself" unstintingly; and I give myself as much to me as to the others. The love that makes my giving possible is their gift to me. This happened last night with A.W., B.B., and S. I don't know whether I "talked too much" or did anything "silly"; I know and knew before we'd started that they were happy in my company. Of course we did pleasant things—danced to old jazz, told stories, exchanged unmalicious gossip, made each other laugh with quips and quotations. All that might have made us nervous or sad instead of joyful. The unexpectedness of the evening helped—I had planned to see A.W. alone (he may have taken advantage of our meeting to resume a flagging frequentation of B.B.), and one should note that where between three people only three channels of communication exist, there are twice as many with four, a potential doubling of liveliness; and last night at least five channels and possibly all six were open. Furthermore, having B.B. join any company can only be a welcome improvement— no, a welcome addition. On the other hand, if I'd known B.B. was coming and counted on it for days, I can swear that neither my expectations nor my behavior would have become stale. If there is one "explanation" for what happened, it is probably to be found in A.W.'s vast and witty warmth. We spent that time in his place, at home in it as we apparently are in his generous heart. He was most audibly present among us, wit and all, but it was his silent love in which we so happily swam.

New York, 11/2/83

One kind of sadness says: it's over before it's begun. It discounts the future in the awareness that of something about to happen, nothing will be left. This implies that sometimes something *is* left, and if this is no doubt true, it is only so as expectation, never in fact (unless you count letters, marriage contracts, and other testimonials to intentions— testimonials perhaps to that very same expectation). What happens in fact, always, is that nothing is left: the moment is over, the day is over, the meal is over, the movie is over, the circus is over, the embrace is over, the bottle of Chambertin Clos de Bèze 1937 is emptied, the class is over, the course is over and the students are filing out of your life, and life too is over—my father's, Georges's, Bob Auzanneau's—and nothing remains, nothing nothing remains, except me. The change may be less radical than it sounds if I understand that there was never anything but me, and the bottle and the circus and Bob existed in me. As consolation this is guaranteed to not always work. Nothing remains of the embrace, and I sink towards sleep, or look around to see what will happen next. Sometimes this sadness happens next. How can we keep exposing ourselves to such disappointment? What inspired this impossible longing in us for something conclusive? Maybe just the experience that hunger wanted to put a thing inside us, and that desire had a body for its target? To swallow her, to be swallowed by her—two apparently terminal acts whose illusion is more "solid," more durable than steak and her bones no matter how exquisite. I want you and can never have you. You said it yourself: "You're already gone!" So I write these words down, leaving the problem (if it is a problem) intact and unmodified.

New York, 11/3/83

Last night I spent a few minutes on Father Demo Square, on the sidewalk in front of the buildings that include the Caffè Lucca. It was six o'clock, quite dark now that we're back on standard time, but warm —warm for the hour, warm for the season. On the island in the middle of the square, a number of people were sitting summerwise on the benches. This might be the last evening on which they could sit out. The outermost benches of the triangular island face inwards—I noticed this because I wanted to sit looking across Bleecker Street at the Caffè Lucca, and couldn't. The square's designer evidently thought bench-sitters would prefer watching each other to watching traffic, a mistake, I think, not because cars and trucks are nicer than people but onlookers enjoy varied more than static scenes.

The Caffè Lucca lay open to the evening. Throughout my vigil, a black man stood talking to a white man seated at one of its terrace tables. To the south, the window of Avignone's drugstore displayed a large volume opened to a double page of pasted-in prescription labels (signed by Moroni, Peroni, and yet another -oni), and a mobile sculpture advertising Swiss army knives—an oblong vertical block fitted with opening and closing outsized scissors- and knife-blades. North of the café, two bearded barbers in their thirties were razor-cutting the hair of two girls in their early teens. Lace of great cleanliness adorned the door pane and the neighboring window of a tenement building. On the benches in the square both blacks and whites were sitting. Around the corner, in another triangular parklet on Sixth Avenue, all the sitters were black.

New York, 11/4/83

Borges also writes on "squared" paper (is that the only name for it?*), but he never leaves a sentence until he's gotten it right.

A bird returns to the paved area outside my window; it makes me think "fat sparrow." Its markings are all on the tail feathers. The smooth gray head and shoulders, rounding into one shape, remind me of Walter Auerbach's hairless dome.

Last night at Ellen A.'s, as I was talking at the table after dinner, R.M. and A.W. fell fast asleep, their smiling, nay, beaming faces still turned in my direction.

Heard in the receiver, the words "Now there's sunlight on my telephone!" filled me with joy at the communicability of human experience.

In this warm, sunny autumn, the very slowly fading leaves hang on the trees by their fingernails, waiting for the severance of first frost.

My mother asked me to find the classical mythology book she used at school, written by her teacher, whose name was Tatlock. I couldn't find it, and I was angry with myself: I know that a useful book is precious, that a childhood book is precious, and that a useful childhood book is priceless. Starting to write this down, I felt a happy pang and looked up, certain that on one of the shelves facing me I would spot the missing book, and there it was, blue as specified: *Greek and Roman Mythology,* with a bar under the title and "Tatlock" under the bar. (Jessie M. Tatlock, says the title page; also that the book was published in New York by the Century Co. in 1917.) The incident suggests that sometimes writing actually may be useful.

Flowering goldenrod along the edge of the ramp leading into the northbound lanes of F.D.R. Drive: the stems bob resiliently in the wake of each car that passes.

New York, 11/6/83

---

*"Ruled 2 sides," "Grid pad": labels seen at Sam Flax's, March 1985.

When I walked out onto the terrace this morning, a team of street tenders (what are they called?) equipped with two trucks and many tools was eliminating the goldenrod from the edge of the ramp, together with other, mostly dead weeds. Was the cleanup routine, or did the impudence of the high flowers attract the eye of a city official motoring past? Ortega y Gassett says the romantic is delighted by the plants he sees growing on cathedral cornices—is delighted more by the plants than by the cathedral. It's perhaps giving the romantic too much credit to say that he prefers life to art; here in any case the goldenrod on the ramp stands not in opposition to art so much as to the "urgency of engineering"—keeping the traffic moving—and to cleanliness: it has been identified with the more usual, senseless, inorganic streetside litter. And I feel no regrets over the goldenrod's disappearance, even if it provided a pleasant surprise, like a sparrow in the subway. The city should tend its thoroughfares.

The workers on the ramp used tools both manual and mechanized. The tools seemed excessive for the removal of a few poor plants. The principle behind their choice seems to be that to squat and to bend over are bad, that a man should be able to do his work upright. Behold one strong man clawing with a long-handled something (hoe or fork) at the scrumbly balls of dead stem at his feet. Another clips a line of weeds with motor-driven clippers that incidentally send a beer can spinning onto the drive below. In both cases, it would be more effective and perhaps easier to get down to dig and yank. As it is, the roots of the weeds have been left intact. We can look forward to the return of the goldenrod.

New York, 11/7/83

Whatever I write tells my story without my knowing it. What I'm aware of saying, even if it belongs to my story, is not the story I'm actually telling. What I am actually telling is "not that," no, nor *that.* Whatever it is I'm telling will lie beyond (perhaps just beyond) what I say I'm saying, so that it doesn't matter much what I'm saying as long as I keep talking to myself (= writing). That is, it doesn't much matter in itself. What I'm saying does matter in its power to give myself access to the things I don't know I know about myself—the things told in my true story. Thus invented matter can sometimes reveal more than subjects I can remember. The highest achievement would be to invent my entire life so that it would correspond to what has "objectively" happened to me—like Pierre Menard reinventing *Don Quixote* without copying it. Then, as in that case, the reinvented "facts" would differ utterly from my mundane, everyday experience of them. My life would become a dream, or perhaps two dreams: my remembered life and my invented life. Of course this happens anyway. If I read today what I wrote about the goldenrod yesterday and the day before, I see that the "real" goldenrod has disappeared, and with it the team cutting it down. How does this differ from my inventing weeds along a street and then going out and seeing them there? Is there any "thing" for another thing to differ from?

New York, 11/8/83

Junkie's Ballad

This dope makes me feel great
                    —maybe it's you!
They say this coke is straight
                    —maybe it's you!
     There goes the needle in me,
        You suck my cock.
     Which one of you will win me?
        I'm still in hock.
Why do I feel Northumbrian?
                    —maybe it's you!
This grass is pure Columbian
                    —maybe it's you!
                Yes, baby,
                Well, *maybe*
                          it's you.

Lines of verse count extra. I say this because I feel that I'm taking all too easy a way out in replacing my twenty lines of prose this morning: a morning of limpid autumn beauty (not all that limpid—an appealing haze whitens the light) with nothing unpleasant about it except the emptiness in my head, noticed as I searched for a topic to write around.

New York, 11/9/83

Opticians and portrait painters do not look at you through your eyes, they look at the eyes themselves. An eye doctor looks into your eyes, not at them or at you. An eye examination is always bewildering (even when, as this morning with Dr. E., it is executed deftly and kindly, the conclusion drawn from it is reassuring ["Well, everything's just fine"], and best of all the sensible decision is made to "give you as little treatment as possible"). Perhaps a rectal examination (perhaps, too, for women a gynecological examination) can disturb this much, but the penetration of the eye with various lights, the flooding of the eyeball with stinging drops, radically threaten my sense of integrity. Someone has climbed inside my head, armed with a terrific flashlight, and is looking around for flaws. I discover that the inside of my head contains not warmth, light, and bustling life but darkness and emptiness. Light and life were the most fragile illusions. I remember emptying the water cistern at Lans and going down into it to search for a non-existent fissure: my eye socket is like that cistern. The eye no longer exists as a solid, only as a precarious, refractive hollowness. When the tube with blue light was pressed against my pupil, I became that blue light and my fear of it. Of course one shove with that or any other of the kind doctor's instruments would have darkened me forever. I walked away, as often from dentists and chiropractors, feeling that I was a thing, and a poor thing at that.

New York, 11/10/83

Must I at last start thinking about television as a presence in my life? Home again (happily so, the grisly rain, hail, fog, and wind notwithstanding), and for the first time I have this box of hollow light to contend with. The contention differs from what I expected; although I admit that I check the program to find out what will be shown during the day. But sets in other houses used to attract my attention irresistibly; this one— "mine"—doesn't. The glamor (in the old sense of the word) has been drained from the screen. "No thrill . . ." Watching the last half hour of *M* last night confirmed my feeling that movies lose most of their power on television: except for part of Peter Lorre's plea to the jury of criminals, I remained an admirer rather than a participant. What surprised me more was my pursuing other business—reading, learning the exercises in *Stretching*—without being distracted by the image flickering nearby. McLuhan meant something else in saying that television was a cold medium; in his view, the coldness drew our own heat into the image. Have I reacted this way because the television set is my own? Was I hooked elsewhere by the fear of missing something? Here I can dispose of whatever the set has to offer. Is this a replay of the "if it's mine it can't be worth much" gambit? That gambit I so often deploy against myself, out of a suspicion that my experience of things is compromised by some original and inexplicable flaw. I must look again into the television set and notice as plainly as possible what is going on. There, after all, no less than elsewhere, is me.

Lans, 11/28/83

Two nights ago, in bed in the dark, I remembered standing up in the Advanced Action Workshop and speaking: "In making promises, commitment drains away. . . ." I did not at once realize why Roger B. had stopped me. When I did, I felt shame at being so stupid, after 1¾ workshops during which we learned over and over that there are no such objective things as "commitment" (or "mind" or the "it" of "it seems"). After suggesting I use only performative verbs, Roger laughed: "We've been here before, haven't we?" I then made my point: "I notice that I lose commitment when I make promises, and I observe that either I transform it into a feeling ('I'd be delighted to . . .') or I put the responsibility on the other person ('If you like . . .')." I said that much and no more; and I said everything I had to say. I had had a particular problem: giving up a certain "charm," not a personal one but that of a kind of fiction that stands in direct opposition to speech that produces results. "Commitment drained away . . .": more than attributing possibilities of action to abstract and external entities, this attributes to them a second, metaphorical existence that reinforces the illusion of their reality—as if commitment had physical qualities that allow me to describe it as a liquid. "Gloom descended like an oversized bat," "Insomnia waited for me like a squad of gorillas": the sorts of things I say, or write in letters. They imply a demonic world through which I wander in a state of some helplessness, of some innocence: "See how good and sad I am!" and how pleasant, too, and let's spend a little time together (but only a little) sharing our sweet absurd loneliness.

Lans, 11/29/83

I raked leaves for two hours yesterday afternoon (a time of chilling and clearing—I was treated to an orange-green twilight over the western hills), and I performed a new kind of raking "underneath" the usual gathering of brittle brown leaves into heaps: scraping away, from the packed pebbly earth of the road, leaves sodden with many rains and squashed by many tires into a slick layer about half an inch thick. I decided to remove this layer in order to reduce the slipperiness of the road when it snows—something that has cost a lot of time and money since I first moved here. The layer came away easily enough under the broad, flexible tines of my fan-shaped leaf rake. Doing the work gave a satisfaction similar to that of shoveling snow (even if I couldn't play with straight-edged patterns): recreating a clear road from an obscured one. I found in it a secondary usefulness, at least as regards the leaves raked near the house. I piled them for warmth and nourishment around the feet of the rhododendron, the newly planted elders, the not-so-old walnut tree. Farther down the road, between the last steep curve and the Big Spring (*la Grande Fontaine*), I eventually became discouraged at the prospect of so much to do, of not being able to finish the job then and there (why was E.M. so devoted to completing whatever one had started on the very same day?). The sun set, I kept working. As the light waned, I noticed that the road earth was much lighter-hued than the dark brown layer of leaves. Scraping the layer away revealed this lightness, first as streaks, then as spaces. Even in the near darkness in which I continued I could always see what I was doing, what I had done and not yet done, so that I was able to do it all. Goodie.

Lans, 11/30/83

When I picked up Léonore yesterday evening, her friend Delphine's mother, Madame Pecqueur—schoolmistress, ski coach—was limping. She had broken her toes several weeks ago: "ces petits orteils qui fónt un si grand mal." Her little son had had a nightmare; she had gotten up and, not turning on the light, smashed her foot into a door jamb. The toes broken were the fourth and fifth—the smallest, indeed. I said: "The pain must have been unbearable—just stubbing a toe is bad enough." "It was awful. I felt that my foot was falling apart (*s'en allait en morceaux*). After a moment the pain was so terrible I had no choice but to pass out." I think I used the word *inimaginable* as I responded to this. The word is certainly relevant. Listening to her, I had remembered stubbing my toe and mentally multiplied by x, x being the difference between a blow and a fracture. But that was only a theoretical operation. Even my recollection of my own pain was abstract—it fell far short even of the residual pain that made her limp. There exists no way of communicating such intensities, of recreating them (except perhaps in the visionary mode)—cf. R.Q. on the primal headache. Something else also happens. The awareness of our incapacity to feel another's pain makes us invalidate our capacity for compassion: in our comfort, what right have we to be compassionate? We turn away. News of violent accidents, of war's nightmare, of torture (political or not—can it matter much?) at once fills us with the sense of being wretchedly unresponsive, whatever our response may be. We turn away, or turn our (perfectly natural) failure to co-suffer ("sympathize") into a question of principle, and that means finding someone or something to blame—Pinochet, God, luck. Only when someone we love (or we ourselves) do the suffering do we begin to act, realizing that talk is useless, the more so because it issues from this sense of our failure, which does not belong to us but to language.

Lans, 12/1/83

Last Sunday—the second day of the two-day OuLiPo seminar in Amiens—I left our hotel a little before nine o'clock to visit (or rather revisit) the cathedral. I went in the front entrance, taking only a brief look at the façade since I did not know how long my tour of the interior would last, and I had to be back at the hotel by a quarter to ten. The interior overwhelmed me—I expected it to be overwhelming, but also to be different from what I found, so I was in fact overwhelmed. Ideas recalled from previous visits and exhumed from what I had once learned about Gothic architecture (the appropriateness of the fifteenth-century organ; the way one's attention is raised by the pointed arches and the height of the building) kept inserting themselves between what I was seeing and what I felt and thought, as if to ward off feeling and thinking as unnecessary dangers. So I made a decision not to think or feel in a special way; although I couldn't help concluding that my reaction to the particular articulation of the space in which I found myself lay virtually beyond my choice, and that one potent element in this "overwhelmingness" was incorporated in the initiatory effect of the ranks of ogives, which depended somehow on the resemblance of an ogive to a cunt. I then went out by the north portal, looking back at it a while from the street opening in front of it, went around the apse to visit the bishop's park and palace (with its spread-armed, welcoming little flight of steps at the door; the palace is now a commercial institute), at last returning to the big clear space at the foot of the west front, which I now spent a few minutes considering. Again I was overwhelmed: not by initiatory exaltation but by mass and number. Arrayed in front of me up and down a congealed, compact wall of black and gray stone were ranks of kings and saints, warriors and saints: the Church Militant. I had wondered before if this cathedral, like that of Albi, could be read as a political statement: I had my answer. The army of figures facing me stood for power—for worldly power. Who would have dared take them on? It seemed to me that if I had looked at them first of all, with the awe I now felt, and then proceeded into the exaltation of the space inside, that exaltation could only have confirmed the power. It would have been an initiation into the knowledge not of Christ but of the Church. I would have twice learned humility and thenceforth obeyed.

Lans, 12/10/83

First snow: I watched it falling, and fallen, without wonder. I was disappointed but not dismayed. Snow as snow, or what happens in this season. What I might have missed was wonder at the world being transformed, a wonder abetted by the silence of its fall and its lying-stillness. I inevitably asked myself: growing old? Now I suggest that I have only lost an unregrettable hope that no longer interests me. A snowfall is not so much a transformation as a Christmas wrapping around a necktie. Longing attaches to the wrapping (oh, what's inside?), not to the tie. I remember the liberation of recognizing that the beauty of Venice was theatrical. I can enjoy the prettiness of the wrapping and give up the longing. Snow resting on branches to turn the treescape into a vividness the blur of bare dull branches can never manifest. Particulars are also no less delightful than before, like the mild scrunch of packed snow underfoot. As for the branches, they provide their best moments when in the woods the snow is shaken from them and they surge upwards from their weighted dip to resume summer angles. This happened several times yesterday while I was exploring a forgotten narrow path up the hill and found myself threatened with snowfall-on-neck. I recalled skiing through trees, being stopped by a bough not only weighted but bent right down to foot level, with its tip frozen into the snow crust, until with a knock of my ski pole the bowed living wood springs free and whooshes upwards, scattering icy powder on all sides, sometimes onto my neck, but at such times I no longer care, and I slide ahead into the next clearing or up to another snowbound branch. Overhead between the treetops I see regions of sky as dark and luminous as the silk of any necktie.

Lans, 12/12/83

I have nothing to write in particular, I'm writing these lines because of my rule that I must write them. I know that I want to get back to writing the last chapter of *Cigarettes.* Yesterday I wrote four and a half pages, and keeping that momentum until Christmas (I reckon I can use nine of my available days, keeping two for buying presents and for other forgotten but inevitable chores that Christmas imposes) will get the chapter done—the first draft of my novel done. There are only bits of other "material" hovering on the edge of my thinking. Bits of dreams: last night, crossing a city intersection, finding or erecting a tent with a regular toilet inside it, into which I copiously shat—image of a great serpentine turd, with a smaller serpentine form at first wriggling then only fluttering around it, which I resolved, to my relief, from snake into tomato skin. And the night before—no, that's lost to me now. Then: I found a sign yesterday as I cleared the piles of paintings and other pictures on the upper level of my study, stating: "Le Temps, c'est de l'argent. L'EXACTITUDE est la première qualite dé L'OUVRIER CONSCIENTIEUX. Remarquez! Ce sont toujours les mêmes qui arrivent en retard." I've hung the sign opposite my desk, for a laugh and also as a reminder, although I'm not sure of what. Needless to say, the "toujours les mêmes" led me to think: me—even though I've been generally on time for years (usually *just* on time . . .) I thought this morning of writing here a list of reasons someone might give for arriving late for an appointment, concluding with "And anyway I'm actually not late at all." But that would be a skit to compose at leisure—time not to be taken this morning. I don't want to be late for my appointment with my novel. I want to be an *ouvrier conscientieux,* no matter how much time I dispose of. So now, having cleared my throat . . .

Lans, 12/13/83

Yesterday evening, having after months of to-do listing bought a new handle for my big pickax, I fitted it to the pick head and set it to soak in the bathtub. (The head was too large for any basin or pail I have.) The union of pickax and bathtub looked strange enough to suggest a "significance" of the umbrella/ironing board type, and I took a Polaroid photograph of it. I had no flash, the film had stayed in the camera since last summer, recently in coldish (3° C) conditions—I'm trying to explain the results before describing them, which is a little like getting the dishes washed before dinner. What appeared on the three-by-three image bore no resemblance to the subject or to anything else. Perhaps to a bent glowing tube, or a grooved, swerving edge of a saddle or a butterfly chair, but there clearly exists (as one looks) no tube, saddle, or chair, only shapes, colors, shading, which nevertheless look like representations of real objects. It is hard for me to stop staring into this undecipherable image looking for a solution, knowing perfectly well that what I'm staring at can only be a chemical accident. I suggest that this image provides a model for the poem: an object that inspires desire while making clear from the start that it contains nothing to satisfy (only nourish) that desire. — Later on, before going to bed, once again considering the pickax in the half-filled tub, I found it most sympathetic, like a new pet just brought into the house and obliged to spend a night or two in these special conditions so as to be domesticated. The beast is curious but not utterly foreign. One must understand its shape as the product of epochs of genetic simplification, the body now smoothly elongated into pure, straight shaft, the head subsumed by what were formerly its appurtenances, the black, now asymmetrical horns.

Lans, 12/14/83

The fun about things, as about thoughts, is getting them, not having them. They become obvious once you have them, just another part of a familiar landscape. Two days ago I came across my course notes about the imaginary reader—the one the writer invents to listen to his imaginary narrator, and on whom the actual reader eavesdrops—and because I'd forgotten the notion I enjoyed a moment of mild excitement reunderstanding it. But after a moment it was back on its rack among the dusty bottles. This has also happened with what I bought myself yesterday (a day mainly devoted to the purchase of Christmas presents): a tape deck, a cassette rack, an outdoor winter country jacket. I nailed the rack into place last night; the tape deck, having been adequately studied in the instruction manual, has been installed in its definitive place; the jacket hangs on a peg by the front door as if it had been there for years. All three will certainly provide convenience or pleasure in coming days as they are used, but the wonder disappeared from them as soon as they were unwrapped and their price tags removed. The wonder grew from the expectation that they would change something in life (how nifty having one's cassettes so handily arrayed, how delicious acceding to glorious music by slipping cassettes into the deck, how warmly glamorous walking outdoors in a bronze-colored, ring-necked, thigh-long jacket). But "of course" I know that expectation is the stupidest kind of lure. . . . What I know too is that the pleasure of buying the things was a real and sufficient one: the pleasure of giving presents and of allowing oneself to be their worthy recipient.

Lans, 12/17/83

For many consecutive days I have only looked into mirrors to see what is familiar—that is, in order not to see. When I shave, I watch the lather coming off my chin, not noticing the chin unless it's nicked and bleeds. Brushing my teeth, I look briefly straight into my eyes, not noticing my eyebrows or the soot smudges on my bathrobe. Having dressed, I look at the collar of my turtleneck shirt to make sure that it is neither too high nor too low, not noticing that my fly is unzipped. If I continued in this way without reminding myself that a closer inspection is necessary, hairs would grow out of my nose and ears, I would gain twenty pounds unawares (this once happened in my late twenties), revolting stains would discolor my teeth, I would wear clothes spotted, torn, years out of date. Using mirrors in this reassuring way leads to blindness of a dreamy sort. It doesn't have to. It is wonderful after a night of dismaying dreams and waking worries that have left me feeling like a loosely connected cluster of shabby objects to look into a mirror and see that I'm whole and, if red-eyed and tousled, unmarked by symptoms of disintegration. Perhaps I can wait until a safer moment to look at myself critically (remembering to look behind, too—backside disgraces otherwise survive literally for years: because of a reluctance to take a backward glance, I wouldn't believe how much hair I was losing until most of it was lost). And while checking myself out, why not notice the nice things, too? The other, blind mirror-looking turns on a pivot that lets the dream that I'm safe inside my body swing out to include the whole world: my body isn't something to be looked at but a medium for being, where I make myself feel as good as I can, not a thing, not a mechanism, not anything real: and after the body, the rest of the world. This can lead to painful surprises.

Lans, 12/19/83

When I brought Emilie home from her school dance last night, Marie asked me, as soon as she saw me, if anything was wrong. I said no, but this wasn't true; more exactly, nothing was wrong, and I was prey to a mild and gloomy irritation. This had begun on the way to Villard, reached its peak in the school parking lot as I waited for Emilie, and was now waning—or at least, like a watchdog trained to growl at particular provocations, was back in its kennel. Since I had insisted on picking up Emilie, I assume the irritation was one I wanted, and at the same time I busily denied to myself that I was indulging it, especially at its strongest: this was when I watched the young men and women walking out from the dance, past the car in which I waited, not wishing them to see me (their looks meant, there's a parent come to pick up a daughter or son), or challenging them by staring back at them. My look meant: my parties, my evenings, my romances are the real thing, you're only playing at playing, I know how to use pleasure and desire and you most certainly don't, you're only beginners—you may think I'm old and out of it but it's you who are out of it. Is there anything more deliciously hopeful than going to a dance when you're fourteen or seventeen, dressing up (this can mean a carefully chosen "casualness"), waiting, leaving the house, entering rooms where the games of desire, usually so inner and hidden, can now be played openly? I'm doomed to deny those evenings their beauty—the beauty not of what's seen but of what's looked for—because that is a backward dream, and who has the nerve to "fondly remember" his youth? I'm six years old now and looking ahead as passionately as ever. My father felt this way, too. I remember *his* irritation at my late night returns, and much later at my sexual adventures; they implied (they didn't, but perhaps *I* did) that he was "beyond" such things. Who wants to be beyond any part of life? Now I can love him for his stubborn youthful impatience.

Lans, 12/20/83

Climbing trees can't provide the delight for French boys and girls that it does for Americans, that it did for me. Is this because of the way the trees here are tended? Wayside trees that grow tall have their lower branches cut away, and in public places even their top ones—as if more shade were given by a profusion of thin sprouting branches than by thicker but fewer old ones. At the edges of woods trees are often cut into coppice, which makes for poor if not impossible climbing. I don't know what happens in the lovely tree parks that customarily adorn *maisons bourgeoises* in country and suburb. In any case, I never see children perched in trees or hear about their falling out of them. For me tree climbing was an exalting joy. I loved it so much it became one of the few physical activities where I lost my clumsiness. Whenever I arrived with my parents at a new house, I would start looking around for a high tree to do my stuff in (in part, no doubt, out of a desire to frighten my elders). With a little time I could recall and describe several particular trees— for the moment they are subsumed in the most wonderful of all, a huge red maple (conceivably a copper beech) on Murray Taylor's estate above the Connecticut River, in Connecticut near Middlesex. I climbed it so high, so easily that I became inexpugnably happy: elsewhere, safe, unique. My father and mother (they used to go there in late May to celebrate a wedding anniversary they shared with the Taylors) looked up at me from far below, anxious, I knew, but helpless, reduced from eternal, looming giants into toy-size people. At such moments I felt full of love for them (in addition to more vindictive sentiments). For once I was sure of being stronger than they, invested with a power that might protect even *them*.

Lans, 12/22/83

I think (and only think, having only haphazardly reread these daily gigs) that what they lack is a sense of how much I love life. I'm afraid that when I sit down to write them, in the state of gentle trepidation that precedes "seriously" putting pencil to paper, I look for minor, self-deprecatory problems to discuss and explore. Even if full of enthusiasm for the day and for my work, I don't leap into the bath of exuberance (*se jeter à l'eau* attractively expresses such an impulse). No doubt I usually don't know where my little problematic subject will lead—I may end up with a glimmering discovery of possibility—but the subjects themselves do begin little, and the possibility only appears beyond them. It is as though I were determined to withdraw at the start to the edge of life: yes, it's all there, but first I must tidy up this junk. The junk generally isn't felt as an immediate burden. I have to look around for it, to find an excuse for not letting fly, for not letting myself fly. (A similar caution perhaps makes one commit oneself imperceptibly but instantly to the manner of another writer when one starts scribbling away in automatic writing.) This resembles my feeling, in response to Elizabeth Cowan's hypothesis that we absorb the life of the familiar dead, that what I must absorb is their weaknesses, their neuroses, *their* junk rather than their particular genius. It's as though there really were in "I" a little *i* that felt in danger of being wiped out, rather than above all the I who am us and you and the unguessed you: an infinity of infinitely powerful creators.

Lans, 12/23/83

Today I can write about one subject only: finishing the first draft of *Cigarettes*. Whether or not, on this last day before we leave for a week in Malta, I actually reach the end of the action (to be followed by the several "distanced" pages with which I began writing the book), I've come to a threshold leading out of the book. Working now is exciting and, because of the weightiness of what is happening, scarier than ever. I've been working steadily and fast for the last two weeks, averaging four manuscript pages a day, about three and a half typed. So much time has passed since I undertook the "writing down" of my stories (themselves so long in crystalizing out of the abstract scheme with which I began) that I cannot believe the process is ending. It will be very much an ending, with no place to go on to. My characters have died or have been delivered into utterly set or utterly changed lives. Some day I must look at these characters, at what a character is, at differences between my characters and those of other novels; at why I hardly think about them as characters. Right now I consider them as marvelous opportunities for inventing particular acts (acts of language, I know, but for the first time overtly connected to behavior determined by an explicit psychological history). Their particularities will become sharper with revision, but their potentiality has accompanied me from the start; and so I can say I shall miss them, and Elizabeth's death will provide a real closure. Do people fill our lives so differently from these ghostly sets of possibilities? The long working out of each character's situation and the coordination of those situations will be missed, too, the way one misses the encounters and interchanges of a place long lived in and then left. Ending a novel: like leaving Venice and a life entire, if not unique.

Lans, 12/24/83

Three days in Malta, the first sunny and still, the next two smitten by mighty winds—yesterday the *majjistral* from the northwest, which had shifted when I parted the curtains this morning to the northeast (the *grigal*). Wherever the wind blows from, it's made life outdoors hard (and indoors, too, until we learned that sliding glass windows and doors must be shut in one of the two possible ways they allow—rubbered edges against frames—and that the air-conditioning unit can produce heat, albeit heat loftily dispensed along the ceiling, far from our cold feet). We managed to persevere inside the high, blond walls of Mdina after buying Léonore a sweater and protecting Emilie's neck with my neckerchief; but after lunch, heading towards the northern edge of the town, we were so buffeted we had to turn around, reactivate ourselves with espressos and brandy at a café facing the bus stop, and take No. 80 back to Valetta and our hotel, whence we have not reemerged eighteen hours later. There has been thunder since dawn, and a few minutes ago a grand shower of hailstones that streaked diagonally through the air at blurring, wind-propelled speed. Does any of this matter? I will not force myself to look at the beauties of this extraordinary island under gray skies in a wet wind, even though I may never come back here and I would love to see them; I know it would be worse seeing them in such conditions than not at all. That's what I learned turning back after lunch in Mdina, a miraculous place. Our half visit would have been poisoned retrospectively if we'd gone on. For what we missed, I reread the few lines in the Blue Guide; and I then read the rest of the guide for the rest of the island: "Malta" is now a detailed object of my curiosity and enthusiasm, a prospect abundantly present in my life. Is there more to ask of any place? Can we ever "miss" anything?

Floriana, 12/28/83

I ask you: what kind of pain did you feel when R.N. turned on you (if that is what he did) in the middle of an apparently vague discussion of awareness and ways of knowing, on the evening of January 26th? You were sitting around the dinner table, I think dinner wasn't yet over, a lot of wine had been drunk (and if R. had drunk more than he usually does, so much the better if this let him vent his spleen). My only note about what happened reads: "an unpleasant talk with R., who turned into an angry missionary preaching that mind is all, and that mind is will." You were maintaining that a not-mind awareness exists that perceives mind and mental experience along with all other experiences (your "Ultimate Ear"). Did R. feel you were attacking him? He said more than once, "You're trying to get me angry at you." The messages you received were: from "the mind is all," that you are living in a state of delusion; from "the mind is will," that you are living irresponsibly out of weakness and will pay for your weakness. I suppose, for starters, that the pain you felt was one of betrayal—you had left yourself open, trusting your friend, and he had taken unfair advantage of you. (Perhaps "for starters" isn't right: it was after the realization that you were being attacked that you began trembling at the thought *he* was attacking you.) A particular factor: being betrayed is an old racket of yours—your excuse for isolating yourself from the world; and R., like Georges, encourages you to participate in the world's opportunities. The next day you thought of reasons why R. might resent you—your money, his owing you money, the apparent ease of your life and your enjoyment of it, your having witnessed his despair last year. His harshness became more bearable as an expression of his feelings right now. Another question remains: did he have any notion of the pain you felt at his words?

Lans, 2/20/84

Doodleyak oh spit comes to whatever part of incidence in the gray ftizhel of morning lamplight and what the incidence may be is what concerns the velpes and shleppes of unknown pferdlike bazzles. So the lines go kalumphing along the chart of Berge-ian graphs until all the factorials are realized and John O'Connor may go back to his diving board. Whatever else you may say about Calvin O'Connor's family they're good boys and girls—one of the younger girls that's to say about twenty-two which is beneath my confidence level is soothingly appealing to the nerd in everyone. I grow by stages—the same stage over and over again. And I find the trouble with this mode is that it gives you too much time to think. Some day make a complete list of all them, the dears. No one to be embarrassed. Absolute dismay of thinking about past touchings. So we gallop backwards into the onwards future and that is where poetry intervenes—poetry *can* be a salvation. Not saving us, saving our words. Our words our words—saving words. Ours O.K. my. So the nincompoop lapped sugared milk out of a can on the back stoop of a front line of embattled semidetached residences; to which return miners, camionneurs (all frizzled and frosty) and a few scouts from the bureaucracy. I live there happily enough. I stay home during the day and fuck the workers' wives. This way I know all about those burly men and when the revolution comes I'll fuck *them*.

(automatic writing)

Lans, 2/21/84

Choosing the next book to read resembles choosing a restaurant or the next Italian town to visit: none ever seems quite right. You want something that corresponds perfectly to your desire, and you can't identify that desire until you find what arouses it. (Thus Venice, before you lived there, was perpetually the next Italian town: a theater of desire, a mirror that promises to reveal, and does—but never definitively.) Today, after finishing *The Reef,* you asked yourself, what next? Marie suggested Danielle Sallenave's collection of short stories—something you certainly want to read, but today you could not look forward to it. You wanted something newer, something about which your expectations were more indefinite. But if *Summer* or *The Age of Innocence* had been available, you would have chosen them with gusto. Can you say this only because they were not available? Or might it be that, as you have been living so much "inside" Edith Wharton's work, within that perspective any unread part of it promises to be unfamiliar? As an indication to the contrary, you noticed how you hesitated to begin an unread novel by James or by Queneau, whose worlds you also know, even better, and whose unexplored regions you know cannot fail to excite. What do you want from a book? No: what do you want from choosing a book? To stand on the threshold of the unfamiliar, the inevitably familiar viewed unfamiliarly, the known capabilities of language yielding opportunities for you to react to them (to reinvent them yourself) with breathtaking, with breathgiving wonder. Choosing: a desire for initiation. Like a first night with a woman; like first reading Marcel Blecher.

Lans, 2/22/84

Remember to notice the advent of absolutely desirable weather (not necessarily *good* weather). Last week's clear cold days—what you recall as being the glory of Vercors Januaries and Februaries when you moved here—have given way to something even better: snowfalls of three and four inches that covered the hard foundation of earlier snow with a soft, elastic surface that skiers dream of. The downhill skier now finds enough substance to turn on without edging; he can, to the side of the pistes, explore possibilities of skiing in less-than-deep snow that still affords a sampling of deep-snow difficulties and delights. The cross-country skier now has something for his skis to bite into when he has to climb. The ski tourer enjoys the pleasure of laying down his tracks without skittering over snow too frozen or sinking too deep into too melting a softness. Other attractions: a night and a morning when every twig and branch of every shrub and tree hung encrusted in creamy whiteness—it looked as though applied by a set designer or a pastry cook; pure fun of clearing the fresh falls—most could be disposed of with broom-like sweeps of the snowshovel. Unless you were smitten with perverse longing for palm trees and warm seas, for the sociable life of a city, or, on the pistes, for having the world utterly to yourself, nothing could be complained about. Every step outside—even drives through the gleaming winter landscape, sometimes blurred with mist or glowing dully under a thin overcast—has proved the desirable inevitability of winter. And of course it won't, as no one quite dares say, last: half frosts will follow half thaws, north winds will torment us under gloomy gray skies. So relish this.

Lans, 2/23/84

In bright late-winter sunlight, your mail sits on a neighbor's window-sill, leaning neatly stacked against the window. The child gets out of the car to fetch it. Back at the house, you take the envelopes and packages and open them eagerly, almost (but you are a grown-up and know better) feverishly. What will those sealed contents reveal? What changes small and great will they bring to your life? Questions both foolish and irresistible. As if something might change, as if the postman (now a briskly efficient young woman) might deliver to you the message, the ultimate message that you've been waiting all your life for, that would make your life clear and complete. Sometimes the ultimate message is in fact received. It reads, more or less: "Your ligament issues from a spa that is given various narcissisms at various time-tables: lozenge, credulity, goggles. And not only your ligament (and that of others): the prodigy that generates mayday has the same orthography. You and the upkeep are one. Give up sugarbowls." At such moments you realize, and you remember, that such messages have never been lacking, and that they are all the same, and that the problem (if that is the word) doesn't involve receiving but deciphering what is received again and again, day after day, minute after minute.

The letter that made you happiest recently (someone planned to devote an issue of his magazine to your work) was opened without such expectation, without expectation of any kind. You found it deposited in your mailbox unusually early on a gray morning in Paris, where your important mail is rarely sent, on your way out to breakfast, still numb from sleep.

Lans, 3/6/84

The elements of inspiration and realization manifest themselves in the interaction of breath and body.

The reverence of instigation and rubberization man-fist themselves in the attraction of braid and Bobby.

The rubberness of dictation and rabbinization—Mom fits the shelves in the refraction of broad and baby.

The lover less of his fixation than rabbitization mops up the shells of the contraption of bores and crazies.

Another mess of civilization or Babbitization crops up in the smells of the collapsed son of mores and laters.

The wateriness of syllabification and babbling nations stops helping middle-of-the-collar paeans of moron haters.

The watery stress in vilification and warbling gnashings starts gulping piddling dollar paunches with morning haste.

A daughtery dress with millinery creations and baubles of fashion parts yelping siblings on their haunches with a yearning for taste.

Slaughterhouse business with milling pulsations and foibles and passions puts mellow twins dribbling under quorums to learning their fate.

More to douse flimsiness in filling pusillanimous joys with crass tootsie jello, the prince jiggles fonder forms and turnip rates.

A fourth mouse limned in stiller establishment poise (and a mute fellow) pinched little Fonda's norm and turned to paste.

A dormouse in chill banishment pays futile homage to get a panda's scorn—the term was "pest."

Dormers instill replenishment—a way of footing language to utter Barleycorn words with zest.

Former millers a-plenty in the gay pussy-lingus of nutty bars earning awards for sex.

Farmer Muller, like twenty in the hay, hustles linkage of Potiphars with swards in Sussex.

Famagusta, intent on pay, misses brinks of poppies and swathes of success.

From a gust of spent wave issue dinky mops and paths of mess.

For adjusted expense, save little ink tops and halves of less.

The busted fence made litter and flops of calves and heifers.

Dust sets pale bits on the caps of cops and vets.

Lans, 3/7/84

If you decided to decode the "ultimate message" of two days ago, you might find the task less forbidding than it at first seemed. Encoding and decoding mean substitution: as a first step, replace all words in the message that strike you as obscure with their most likely dictionary definitions. The message then would read: "Your connecting bond issues from a mineral spring that has attributed to it various [forms of] excessive love of yourself, according to the listings of various arrivals and departures: pleasantly flavored medication; gullibility; protective tinted spectacles. And not only your connecting bond (and that of others): the fearful event that generates [your] signals of distress manifests the same method of representing sounds by literal symbols. You are one with the maintenance [of things] in proper operation, condition, and repair. Give up your covered sweets." — You already have been provided with more accessible meanings. The very process of discovering and transcribing started possibilities of interpretation flashing in your imagination: the "mineral spring" seemed to appear for the exact purpose of reflecting Narcissus. . . . Much, if not all, of the message can be read as an injunction to give up pleasurable escapes (cough drops, dark glasses, sugar) and to accept the conditions of existence. Those conditions frighten you, but they also give you your life. That the conditions include a *mineral* spring and that you are connected to the "proper operation" of what is outside you imply a link with the inorganic world that remains hard to grasp. Furthermore the "method of representing sounds by literal symbols," common to what binds you to the world and to the frightening event, demands investigation.

Lans, 3/8/84

To push the "ultimate message" farther: the "minerality" of the spring, the fact that it *is* inhuman, in itself explains why the narcissisms you saw in it *were* narcissisms (a kind of pathetic fallacy) and why you were overcome by an urge to escape from the fact of your origins into the several consolations mentioned. On the other hand, the bond and the fearful event, which issue from the spring, both lend themselves to literal symbolic representation: so that here you have access to the variety and unity of your own history; and mightn't it be possible that through your attentions to the symbolic representations of origin and history you maintain "things" (everything? the universe? *your* universe?) in functioning order? But what about the element of sound— "sounds" are what the symbols represent. What are the sounds of your origin and your history? Perhaps an explosion cracking the rock and allowing the spring to rise; the moving water; screams of pain or fear. But what of the silence before that, the silence flooded with white or blue-white light, or with whatever the light emerged from? Silence cannot be represented, but it can be implied by sound, and so pure empty light can be inferred from literal marks on a substantial surface, through whose blankness you stare into shifts and upheavals of unwritten questions. The point (*a* point): this looking through, this looking back ("back" only because of the convention of time: it means looking at you right now) holds such satisfaction that you can give up your terror and your sweetened distractions. You can admit birth, you can admit death, because they are one, and the one is you.

(NB: Your being made of matter means that matter has your intentions.)

Lans, 3/9/84

Having nothing to write about (nothing *particular* to write about) suggests a question: what this morning do you particularly not want to say? Think of the abundant opportunities for flight you've had since yesterday afternoon, and after asking yourself which of them may conceal this specially avoided "danger," ask yourself what else had been going on? There was the painful case of Françoise G.'s health: to be left simmering in the multiple discomforts of a malfunctioning thyroid gland—insomnia, anguish, failures of energy and will, not to mention indigestion—provided in itself an upsetting prospect, all the more so for its reminders of N. in the midfifties. (Can you face your willingness then to put up with horrendously callous and ineffective medical treatment?) And your dinner with the G.s, so incomparably warm and kind (and no fools): where did your responsibility lie when the conversation stayed so conversational (what have you been doing and what are your plans? and the dead horses of promotional mafias and the power of advertising!). And your incredible fantasies about E.: she would behave so abominably to you that you could justify a coldly furious expulsion—send her to boarding school. There! So much for you! And that this could only refer to your Mother, that fictitious beast—what did you think of yourself when you poured her over-powering Nature into the mold of an adolescent girl? Are you sometimes worried that you may be literally insane? Well—what *are* you so worried about?

Lans, 3/10/84

Each day happiness lies in wait for you around unpromising corners. Conceivably, if you weren't careful, it could surprise you at every moment—how could you possibly survive that? Yesterday, which was yet another in the present succession of dazzling mornings and middays (and this time the cloudlessness lasted round the clock), cold as January but brightened with the intenser sun of March, you agreed to go ski touring with E. The prospect was neither exhilarating nor discouraging; but you knew you were setting off with a fourteen-year-old girl who could be difficult and demanding to the point of petulance. You would be facing climbs and descents that two days ago had been difficult enough to dismay you, even though you had known more or less what to expect. Yesterday, it's true, the heat of the sun had softened the snow, making climbing slopes on the trail less laborious and coming down them slower and so less demoralizing. Still, the going was often strenuous and the outing long—more than two hours virtually without pause. E. remained a joy to be with. When she complained it was matter-of-factly, or because—as when her foot was inextricably twisted under her—she experienced pain. Most of the time she stayed in an equally matter-of-fact way not only willing but enthusiastic. She responded without prompting to the loveliness of the passage through the open birch wood, to the spread at its end of shining fields overlooking the plain before Villard, to the pleasures of navigating the trail I had opened earlier in the week. When we came to the very steep descent down to Les Replats, she overcame her anxiety and fatigue and kept her skis on all the way to the bottom, several bad spills notwithstanding. I had nothing to do but enjoy her. Except perhaps once: when we had gone a ways along the new trail Idelon had suggested, she remarked, "No way of telling where we are," and I sensed she was afraid we were lost; and I then did the right thing—I ignored her.

Lans, 3/12/84

Liz I. phoned last night to let me know that Douglas Harding, one of the Zen masters of the west, was soon coming to Paris to lead a weekend seminar. I had no reservations, or no conscious ones, about participating until she mentioned that there would be translators translating; I then turned lukewarm. Perhaps in part the idea of translation simply breached my awareness and allowed suppressed objections to surface; but it triggered a specific anxiety. Translation means making knowledge and experience available to those to whom they would otherwise remain inaccessible; that is, translatable knowledge is not privileged by particular, private aptitudes. If it's translatable, anyone can get it. To me this implies that I was dismayed by the prospect of learning something that I have no excuse for not knowing; that for all I *have* learned, the essentials still remain to be learned, and that living as I do "between revelations" is only living on the strength of dead experience—living on concept. Furthermore, the instinct to turn away from an opportunity such as spending a weekend with Douglas Harding means inescapably that I'd *rather* live in a state of unawareness, of stumbling along, of not knowing or more precisely of not knowing that I don't know: as if unconsciousness, in my case at least, brought a certainty of overriding all those times when I touched the inspiring duality of things-are-what-they-are and the-power-of-the-universe-is-mine.

Lans, 3/13/84

Having survived falling out of bed, smacking his head, cracking two vertebrae, spending several weeks in the hospital, and returning home yesterday morning, François L.L. died during the afternoon. He had "eaten normally," then, while talking to his secretary, felt indisposed ("il a eu un malaise"), and that was it. P.F. phoned me the news in the course of the evening.

I felt real loss, much more of a one than I had anticipated. Obvious explanations—the OuLiPo and I have lost a founding father; the deaths of the past three years have left me vulnerable to death in general— could not account for my feelings. My surprise at them, at least, was easily explained. F.L.L. had always shown me kindness and attention but no affection other than the "impersonal" kind dependent on our membership in the OuLiPo. Similarly, he admired my work without ever responding to it as an act of poetry. This attitude had nothing to do with me. He did not really ever enjoy writing except as a demonstration of ideas that interested him, and where I and, for instance, G.P. were concerned, the same could be said of his relations with people. He was a powerfully self-centered man, incredibly knowledgeable, no less productive, with others not cold so much as distant, with the distance that springs from an extraordinary concentration of will and talent on the pursuit of a few abstract and complex goals.

What a wonderful way to live! Francois must have had great satisfactions every day of his life; and not only in intellectual accomplishment. Men and women of the finest sort came to him with their affection as much as with their esteem. His brilliance never cut him off from our human presence: if he was distant, he was always generous. And he had the strength not only of his convictions but of his courage. If I'd been made prisoner with him, I too would have entrusted him with my life.

I needed his death to learn that I loved him.

Lans, 3/14/84

Yesterday I drove to Grenoble to order tools that will improve the conditions in which I work: a draftsman's table that can be raised and lowered as well as tilted, together with a complementary "tractor" chair on which to perch intermittently, and an Olympia electronic typewriter. I scheduled the purchase of these long-desired pieces of equipment for this month; if I hadn't, probably another year would have passed without my buying them. Even so, I felt that I was forcing myself to perform a chore rather than doing myself a favor, as though maintaining the less-than-perfect conditions in which I write (a cluttered desk that entraps me, an old portable) were, since I manage to function in them, necessary for my functioning. I forget that writing brings opportunities for discovery and all the satisfaction discovery provides. I mustn't stop now: as soon as I see how the draftsman's table works for me, I should add new tables, high, low, large, or small. My "desire" (is it a real desire or one I think might be desirable?) demands a table or desk for every activity—novel, poetry, essay, workshop, OuLiPian research, and x (say theater, or a second project in fiction, poetry, etc.). I can move from one to another according to the impulse of the moment.

I think I'll enjoy writing standing up; after all, that's how I generally wrote my courses. I know I'll enjoy walking around as I work—the rhythm of walking generates sentences and lines. I must buy a more functional chair, too, than the one I now use, with its slippery straw seat and its arms precisely in the way of my arms as they extend towards the desktop.

Lans, 3/15/84

Tomorrow, if all goes well, you'll finish your book: "only the first draft," but already you are showing symptoms that suggest a term, one that resembles delivery more than deliverance. You are becoming impatient and irritable, you may find yourself soon in a right sulk. In fact after tomorrow, even with much work to do, the book will no longer be something you imagine but a thing written down, outside you; no longer a gestation but an accomplished act; no longer a set of possibilities but a particular realization of them. A child in the womb means life itself; once out of it, a definite, individual brat. What remains to be done—nourishment and "education"—has its interest and importance, but the parent is stuck with a final set of opportunities to watch, and to allow and encourage to develop. Dreams of glory are put aside in the face of small practical imperatives. If ever, glory will come years later, when it will have no connection with the easy, comforting hope that the unborn work generated. You will no longer have the consummate ending, the triumph of your long expectancy, to look forward to. Whether the ending is consummate, or only a promise of consummateness, or a total disappointment will make no difference; or nothing like the difference of bringing things to an end. You will have been emptied: nothing left to wonder about, nothing to reassure yourself with, nothing regarding the absolute realization of your power in language to look forward to. At the same time all this is irrelevant, inaccurate, and ridiculously misleading.

Lans, 3/16/84

Clumsiness, uncoordination, falling, breaking things, hurting oneself: functions of the unconscious, as we know, but more interestingly, functions of the act of *going* unconscious. You start down a steep slope on your skis. Your eyes are open, you feel your legs, and as you give in to speed, your eyes inside you shut, and the feeling of your legs stops being an everchanging responsiveness and freezes them stiff. You still see and feel, but these acts have moved from an active into a passive mode. You have given up the opportunities of seeing and feeling and are now only enduring them as best you can. The active you has withdrawn from your senses and hides in darkness. Now this withdrawal obviously does you no good. It leads to fear, embarrassment, and possible pain. You cannot excuse choosing to withdraw as a natural reaction to the unnatural sensation of sliding downhill on two thin, slippery boards, because often the withdrawal is chosen in circumstances that are static and in no way threatening (for instance, when you tore the skin of your right middle fingertip on a nailhead the other day—you were simply reaching into the back of a drawer, and the nailhead was perfectly visible). At what point does your choosing to withdraw into blindness take place? What suggests the possibility to you? It must happen *before* any unconscious gesture is made; otherwise you would realize that you can remain conscious while performing the riskless gesture, that you can go on seeing and feeling. In other words, you must like going unconscious: you must like being clumsy, embarrassed, and hurt. What a very funny person you are!

Lans, 3/17/84

The weather hasn't changed in the last few days. During the nights the temperature drops to about 5° below zero (C), rising to 2° below at breakfast time and to 4° to 5° above in the early afternoon. The ground is still covered with at least a foot of snow. Sunny mornings usually lead to more or less overcast afternoons—yesterday afternoon it snowed a little, fine wet snow, but still not rain. But the birds have started singing—songs sustained on high perches in the big ash tree or the larches behind the house, not incidental chirpings provoked by sudden encounters. How do the birds know spring is coming? Especially as spring here will mean almost two more months of night frosts and blustery, chilly days? The question isn't entirely one of amazement at the mysterious workings of the natural world: you too can tell the difference. One way of noticing it: when the thermometer rises to 0°, it feels warm and not merely less cold (or, since -5° is generally dryer than 0°, actually "colder"). Yesterday, at such a moment, M.C. announced with evident relief and expectation, "Ah, qu'il fait bon!" You note also the obvious (even to the city-bred) fact of the lengthening span of daylight, so dear to my mother, and another element also dear to her: the kind of light now filling the days. Is it really brighter and warmer and richer in color than midwinter light? Does the lessening of its angle from the vertical make us rise up straighter within ourselves? When it blows, the wind feels as cold as ever, as does the snow when you fall into it, and clouds sweeping over the sun turn the world as dark a gray. But we all know it's springtime; or, at least, time for spring.

Lans, 3/20/84

Having everything in a state of absolute risk provides the condition for staying alive (in the sense of "lively"). Thus performers—actors, musicians, athletes—become our models. That last night's performance of Malvolio was astounding doesn't help the player this afternoon. What good did John Riggs's statistics do him in the Super Bowl? What use was Toscanini's praise to the snare-drummer as he went ape performing the *Boléro?* Earlier today you knew I loved you, and during the evening I said something that cut you out of my life. I wrote something good once; today I don't know what to do on the page. Last week I gave a talk that made listeners think in a way wholly new to them; this time they are watching and listening from a distance. "Mastery is not knowing what you are going to do next"; and "In life there are no holidays." You never have earned the right to sit at the table and let someone else clear away the dishes. No accumulation of knowledge can guarantee that you aren't a fool. The roast is over-cooked. You slice bread for the seven-hundredth time and cut off the tip of your left forefinger. You touch her as coarsely as any boor, being now the boor. You meet an old friend, you have forgotten his name, you cannot look him in the face: not looking him in the face, you wound him and you start lying to him and to yourself. Go off and sulk and complain and explain why it happened. It won't help. Instead, be an actor, or an athlete, on stage, on the field, giving—as you once eagerly proposed to yourself—everything to the perishable act.

Lans, 3/21/84

"I love you, and I want you to know I'll always love you." — I once used the statement "I'm yours forever" to illustrate the effect of ominous pleasure, the ominousness lying in the implicit claim of the speaker to possess the hearer for life. But another ominousness appears in "I want you to know I'll always love you." It shows in the unspoken words that might readily be attached to the spoken ones: "whatever happens." These words imply that something may very well happen, or already be happening; that present circumstances may change. The words thus conjure up a prospect that the natural course of the romance or affair (however the relationship is tagged) is in fact virtually completed. They strike a dirge-like note, one of looking back, possibly happy but no less final, and of reassurance that this change of perspective is not one's fault or, at least, not due to any particular act. For all its kindness, the sentiment sounds conclusive. The kindness only makes the conclusiveness more telling: matters have been moved from the realm of passion, where "anything can happen," to that of reasonable choice. If the person hearing these words is still fervently committed to the mutual love now so sweetly sent to heaven, he will be plunged into a fury of impotence and despair. The best he can hope for is melancholy—he can start gently arranging a funeral for part of his life and of himself. The arts, especially those like music and poetry that are primordially linked with the passage of time, will supply him with words, images, and melodies to decorate his wake. *L'hiver est mort, tout enneigé, on a brûlé les ruches blanches. . . .*

Lans, 3/22/84

For the first time in ten years I find myself in this house alone. The experience has remained unchanged: as before, I am accompanied by an imagined other. Well, it has changed in this respect: most of the time, perhaps all of the time, that other can now be named—the specific M.C. who on Sunday will return here in fact and flesh. But I have re-discovered the unchanged truth that living alone never means quite that, at least not to me. Others may, I imagine, make of living alone a somewhat strenuous point: "There's no one else here," turning that fact into an emphatic absence of one person or several. (Should I reread *Walden?* If Thoreau was truly living alone, for whom was he writing so eloquently? If he was writing for himself, for whom was he publishing?) Living through days and nights here enacts a freedom whose perfection —I do exactly what I like when I like it—provides a model to be shared with or displayed to those I care about (parents, lovers, friends—but not children . . .). This reminds me of going alone to beautiful churches or magnificent museums and there relishing the discovery of some extraordinary work. The direct, enthusiastic experience of the work is helplessly mixed with the hope of telling about it—especially telling the person I might have come with, but didn't. It reminds me a little as well of getting good marks in school, or hitting a home run, or even finding a moment of true happiness, and wanting to go home and put it on display.

Lans, 4/4/84

You are becoming inclined to give up the practice of beginning your writing day by setting down twenty lines on "any subject" once this pad of sixty-odd leaves has been filled. Perhaps the time has come to begin considering what else you might do, remembering that the purpose of the practice is to demystify the act of writing, to demonstrate to yourself that the fears it inspires in you are as imaginary as they are persistent. What else could do this? You can use a few practical criteria. Whatever you do should have a clear limit set to it, so that you will know, however reluctant you may feel on any particular day, that it can be repeated. In addition to being short, what you do should not require a lot of reflection: a five-line poem is short but might need hours to finish. Access to the procedure should be easy, that is, the obstacles to setting down the first line or two should be reduced as near as possible to non-existence. You have the possibility of continuing with your present exercise but setting up the next day's subject in advance, perhaps even writing a first sentence at the end of the daily stint; the disadvantage of this is that it might limit its value as a "journal." You might turn your twenty-line sections into a continuity—a novel, an essay, a description, a meditation. You might write a poem, or rewrite one, not looking at its earlier versions but inventing it anew—aspiring to that spontaneity which experience and discipline can produce, exemplified by the Chinese painter who dashed off a perfect rendering of a cock for his emperor without showing him the room papered with thousands of prior attempts.

Lans, 4/5/84

M.C. wrote me from the Lot to complain about something I'd said to her on the phone Thursday night, and not for the first time: something suggesting that she didn't like this house. She had every right to complain. What I said could be named petty provocation—not only self-indulgent but cruel. ("Not liking the house," which in fact suggested not liking the life in it, made her a foolish victim, something she could never be.) Why have I repeatedly provoked her in this way? In other words, once more: what do I get out of it? Answer: reassurance. I have no real doubts about the house, about living in it (M.C. has spent months here without me). Why should I need such reassurance? Because the house is me, filled the way I am with my past mistakes and the suffering they brought—the crazy way I behaved towards Niki, towards my children, towards Maxine, not to mention myself (remember how many times I've physically wounded myself inside or outside these walls). I feel that I need to be told that these things can be accepted by someone else, although my provocation aims at more than that: a perpetuation of the very mistakes and sufferings for which I want to be forgiven, a reassertion of blindness towards those I love. It belittles them and me. It means essentially that my life remains hopeless, and thus dependent on hope, and that I can neither expect nor deserve love but only a woman's generous forgiveness. Thank you, beloved M., for writing that letter.

Lans, 4/6/84

"Our ancient winter nurses." One was gray-haired and lean, not unkind, never attempting to charm. She assured our survival during bleak days, tending our clothes, our promptness, our sleep. Without her we would never have ventured out of doors, where the north wind threatened to blow people like leaves into heaps in somber stone corners. She made sure we wiped our eyes clear of the sticky secretions of winter sleep. She would not listen to excuses. She hugged us mildly, rarely, bonily. We dreaded her leaving us because we were helpless without her.

Another was small, brown, and jolly. She beamed with the heat of the oven she watched over (the way a smith watches over the coals of his forge). She smuggled warmths to us. She brought us surprises of roast pigeons and forbidden storybooks. She nourished our secrets and our dreams of other, summery lives. She hugged us hard and laughed happily doing it, making us laugh or at least smile, and we could forget the cold that clenched our hands and bowels.

Another was tall, tallest of all, dark-haired, white-skinned, powerful but distant, smotheringly palpable and also so impossible to hold on to she might have been transparent. She brought us honey in hot milk when we lay sick in bed. She listened to our questions abstractedly and gave them abstract answers. She governed our dreams.

Another, gray-haired like the first, but large and almost stately, waited near the door, watching us. She was the fond, hopeless, powerless witness of our disarray, our smallness, our pathetic dissolution among the intractable people and things that surrounded us. When she took us in her arms, her embrace felt sad and gentle, as though it were the last.

Lans, 4/7/84

"These are the first words . . ."—those *were* the first words written on my new draftsman's table, delivered this morning. They were no sooner written than A.P. arrived to install the "parallel rule" (*la règle parallèle*) that is to prevent papers, pads, files, books, and notebooks from sliding off the smooth, matte composition surface onto the floor. The table is a beautiful thing. The writing board is supported on a base consisting of two tubular legs shaped like narrow inverted U's, with a tubular foot running across the mouth of each U, projecting about thirty centimeters beyond it on either side. The legs are connected to the board by an adjustable parallelogram made of bone-shaped pieces of flat metal. The knobs of the bones are pierced with pivotal studs that hold the sides of the parallelogram together. Two strong springs, to hold the angles chosen in place, maintain pressure against two other springs fixed just below the board. A single lever controls this disposition and locks the board in place. Changing the angles of the parallelogram permits one to alter both the height and angle of the board in one movement. Board, parallelogram, legs, and feet are white; springs, studs, and lever handle are black. (The seat of the "tractor stool" that accompanies the table is white also, but shiny white.) A.P. examined the instructions, plans, and pieces of hardware associated with the parallel rule, in my not particularly helpful company. He has now gone home for his drill. He's also promised to bring a sample of wood stripping to screw to the lower edge of the table. The rule, higher up, will provide a restraint for objects resting on its upper edge: A.P.'s stripping will provide an ultimate barrier of whatever may be heading floorwards.

Lans, 4/9/84

Yesterday, a sunny day, I drove up to the Stade de Neige to ski. In a northeast wind, clouds were blowing across the peaks (more exactly, the rim of the plateau), thickest towards the north, thinning out then altogether dispersing as they moved south. I asked A.P.'s brother, who was checking tickets at the bottom of the ski lift of the *I bis* piste, if it wasn't cold at the top. No, only *un peu de brouillard.* In fact the fog was so thick I could scarcely see five yards. I was completely disoriented at the end of the first steep slope, even though I'd skied it dozens of times. Set in the right direction by skiers who passed me, I started down the next stretch, no less steep and bumpy to boot. But I couldn't see the bumps: so I couldn't think about them, only react to them as I crossed them. My body did the thinking. I discovered that there was more resiliency in my legs, more adaptability in my whole body, more skiing talent (in whatever part of me that resides) than I had ever given myself credit for when I was able to see where I was going. I knew much more than I thought I did. Knowledge as foresight or apprehension meant my becoming subject to all the clumsy habits I'd held on to since my first days on skis; whereas letting myself respond in the act to whatever was happening meant knowing what should be done. This has nothing to do with "instinct" or "not thinking." The right "instincts" in skiing differ entirely from those we have as walking animals and can only be learned by experience; and as for thinking, I had never "thought" more cleverly —never for a second was I "letting myself go." There is a liveliness in us that learns what we need to know every moment of our lives. I needed to be blinded by fog to trust it.

Lans, 4/10/84

You have a fantasy of discovering that you suffer from cancer, or a brain tumor, or some other affliction of a most grave, probably mortal kind. You keep the knowledge of it entirely to yourself. Not only do you not burden those who love you with the news, you become for them a companion of perfect humor, gaiety, and warmth. Needless to say, you do not give your "enemies" the satisfaction of knowing you are doomed. Since you can't entirely conceal your condition, you explain the treatment you are obliged to receive as necessary for some less spectacular ill—an infected tooth, an abscess close to a nerve, a bone spur near a sensitive articulation. And so you live out your life to its precocious end with secret (and indeed inwardly modest) heroism.

Your life gives absolutely no credence to this fantasy. Two years ago you felt the first twinges of a strange neuralgia running down the right side of your face from eyebrow to upper lip. You mentioned it at once. The twinges came and went seasonally; now, over the past several weeks, the neuralgia has recurred more and more frequently. You have mentioned it with comparable frequency. And now that it has become a fixture of your life, you are beginning to strike the pose of the doomed victim. You of course find no difficulty in recognizing the single need lying behind this behavior and your apparently contradictory fantasy: an abject desire for pity. *Basta!*

Lans, 4/11/84

So whatever gets in the way, eat it. Don't hesitate for a second thinking of the consequences which may be Fats Waller or the eunuch sprung from the cellars of the harem on the way to political prominence. The point is that resentment leads to torture and that's that. Stay out of the hands of torturers, stay out of the hands of the tortured. Larks leap out of the snow flying backwards into summers neither you nor anyone else is ever going to forgive. The rest, which is a lot, is movies. Sit in your pig(?)covered pigstuffed chair and watch the waves of regret wash over the unreal rocks of your soul. There's time for that when you're dead. Movies for the living dead are composed of equal parts of rose liqueur, pelleted shit, and good intentions. Of course good intentions aren't all bad, only the people who have them. Let's make it all work. Even if it doesn't make sense. The only way you're ever going to get to the bottom of this page is to kill yourself. It won't take long—the long part is the explanation. And that doesn't matter so you can skip it. Then just skip into nothingness, into that post-Pythagorean zero they made so much fuss about. And they were right; except that once nothing is, and so nothing has to be this way or that (how can it?), the problem of choice remains absolute. Well, that sounds like fun. Or funny. Certainly nothing to shed cold cold tears over, while the squirrels scamper away into the maples.

(automatic writing)

Lans, 4/12/84

So you were right to call the pain on the right side of your face a neuralgia: more properly, a *névralgie faciale,* affecting the *nerf trijumeau* or trigeminal nerve, but not the *tic douleureux* (affecting the same nerve) that you so compulsively diagnosed from your medical encyclopedia last Wednesday.* You went to see the excellent local Dr. T., who made sure there was no specific cause for your pain, like sinus trouble, by having you X-rayed. (You made him laugh when, looking at a profile of your skull, you exclaimed, "We really are all alike.") He reassured you. He said that such neuralgias can be effectively treated, and he prescribed a treatment: a month of vitamin B and an anti-convulsive drug called *carbamazépine* (brand name Tegretol) that incidentally and inexplicably calms facial neuralgia. You then began a new life. Your insomnias ended. You sleep long, solid, indeed impenetrable hours. When awake, you progress gently through your day, and calmly, reacting to news good or bad or to the most unwelcome interruptions with an equanimity you have often longed for. You have decided that it is better to avoid occupations such as driving a car or manipulating a chain saw. (Two or three days ago—you are in no condition to say which—you almost backed off a side road into an oncoming car.) You do your best to stagger through the day without injuring or offending yourself or those around you. You are going to call Dr. T. and implore him to take you off this drug. Your facial neuralgia, after all, disappeared three days ago, on Friday the Thirteenth.

Lans, 4/16/84

*Tic douloureux, however, is another name—an English one—for trigeminal neuralgia.

Yesterday you "somehow" forgot to write your twenty lines for the day—something that has never happened before on a writing day (unless you did it deliberately). You planned to do it, noting it on the page of the agenda you fill out each morning, and today you checked it off as something done; then in an afterthought you looked at the date on the last twenty-line entry and saw that it belonged to the day before yesterday. Can you find reasons, i.e. excuses, for this lapse? Yes: you could blame it on the Tegretol you've been taking, even though Dr. T. has allowed you to reduce your dose by a third. (Do you credit Tegretol for your recent beautiful dreams?) More likely something was waiting for you that you did not want to say or face and that you would have had to say or face if you had set your pen to this page. There had, after all, been an unexpected event in your morning: your son P., whose arrival N. had warned you of the previous evening, had already appeared. No matter how little this conforms to your ideas about yourself, you must admit that you felt his presence as an intrusion. More, your attitude towards him signifies something like: you went through the sometimes difficult and certainly long process of making your relationship with him open, generous, and loving, so he could at least do you the favor now of staying out of your life. Ask the old question: what possible satisfaction do you get out of such an attitude (a wholly mean one— mean to yourself in its closing off the possibilities of support and communication on which, as you well know, you thrive)? A provisional answer: since one recreates one's parents in one's children, and your father is dead, you wish P. to be dead. You might remind yourself that if your father is dead, this means that he is alive in you—willy-nilly. Closing your heart to either your son or your father can only lead to your own death.

Lans, 4/18/84

After years of saying how much you preferred cross-country skiing and ski touring to downhill skiing, how making one's own way (and if necessary one's tracks) in its tranquility, its involvement with nature, and its privacy surpasses being hauled by machines up hillsides in the company of other paying customers to be released at the top of prepared slopes, it has been a true joy for you to rediscover the heady pleasures of downhill skiing. Today you went back to the Cote 2000 in Villard for the first time in perhaps twelve years. That was where you had learned to ski, although you had spent a beginner's week at Gargellen in Austria and another at Argentière. Many things had changed since your last time there, mostly for the better. The two-seater eggs have been replaced with four-seater cabins, the snow is better tended, and there are many more and, above all, higher pistes. You went past Les Jaux into a region that you had never before seen close up in winter, between the summit of the Cote 2000 and the Moucherolle: tracts of wooded and then more sparsely wooded landscape interrupted with the great troughs of coombs, between which three tows threaded their small, effective paths (two of them changed directions as they rose) to bring you to the very edge of the plateau. You had this new world virtually to yourself—you saw barely twenty other skiers between 11:15 and 1 P.M. —in spite of its glorious attractiveness: banked sheets of glittering whiteness bordered with spruce forests and outcroppings of limestone or with the cliffs of the Moucherolle and the Rochers du Gerbier themselves; the snow you skied on hard at first, then softening in the blazing midspring sun, as you followed your son Philip, aereal, expert, his movements both unbelievably smooth and unbelievably quick as he led you into this seemingly endless, deliberately created bedazzlement.

Lans, 4/19/84

"Non è Roma, ma quasi," said Gigi, who runs the restaurant across the street. He was referring to the weather (almost 80° in the shade at the moment), in response to your suggestion that you eat outside on the sidewalk, where very small tables had been set up, all of them empty now as they are always. The prospect appealed to you more than sitting in the bottleneck of the strangely shaped restaurant, especially as today few cars were driving down Rue de Varenne, so that you would be spared dust and exhaust fumes. So you sat down outside, alone, although not for long—it was then that the Romanness of your situation began to affect you. The little Neapolitan girl you'd met two nights before and another girl slightly less little (perhaps nine or ten) came out and started playing near you and eventually decided that they too would eat out of doors at the end table behind you. From time to time one of their mothers or fathers would emerge from the interior of the restaurant to see how the girls were doing and exchange a few words with you. The waiters, or rather family assistants, spoke to you in Italian. Little by little, with the properly French life of the street in holiday abeyance (today is Easter Monday), most of the passersby being foreign tourists going to or coming from the Musée Rodin, and the street itself not perhaps particularly Roman in look but of a classical seriousness that might have played a role in some counter-Counter-reformation neighborhood in Rome that you had stumbled on one festal spring day on your way to a remote equivalent of the Musée Rodin, you found yourself sitting in a place not Paris and not Rome but an idea of Rome, as strange and comforting as a description in *The Marble Faun,* which lay closed on your table while you ate and drank.

Lans, 4/23/84

Two hard-working (hard-writing) days were spent without resorting to these pages. Instead of having to warm up, the "problem" became cooling off and stopping. Finishing the revision of *Cigarettes* lay only a few hours away, and a let's-cut-the-crap-and-get-it-done enthusiasm took over. Almost a frenzy: five hours of revising and typing flat out on Wednesday, and on Thursday an agitated, anguish-ridden urge to get the final typing done and the whole typescript Xeroxed. "Anguish" isn't too strong a word, although "anxiety" might be a more accurate one. It would have been possible to go back to P.O.L.'s in the afternoon to finish the Xeroxing, but that was not desirable; what was absolutely desirable was getting it done by lunch. And that was done, at the cost, also desired, mysteriously, of becoming a mechanical puppet linked absurdly to the rhythm of the photocopying machine, a stiff puppet, although a quickly moving one not without a stiff coordination of the hands. When afterwards it came to light that thanks to P.O.L.'s demonstration of a still faster way of getting the paper on and off the machine more than a few pages were blackened or smudged, it made no difference to the accomplishment of the task. Some pages were corrected on the spot, others, discovered later, were replaced at a commercial copy shop—that was then only a part of the post-desiring process of checking and wrapping up. So that there was no dissatisfaction. But in this experience of desire and satisfaction, what happened to "you"? Where is "I"?

Lans, 4/30/84

As you were reading Alix Cléo Roubaud's *Journal* last night, in which she several times mentions going to the BHV to buy what she needs, it occurred to you that people who live near department stores have a peculiar awareness of their "convenience." You yourself when in Paris live only five minutes from the Bon Marché. The convenience— apparently the availability under one roof of virtually everything one might currently want—should be summarized differently: to shop in a department store, you have to walk through only one door. You need stationery, a watch strap, and an extension cord. Buying these items in smaller, specialized shops means passing through three doors, doors that at once confront you with the half welcoming, half mistrustful gaze of the stationer, the clock seller, and the hardware dealer whose sanctuary you have entered. When you pass the impersonal glassed portals of the Bon Marché, which already considerably reduce the separation of indoors from outdoors, no one looks at you, except for a guard or supervisor so discreetly posted you do not notice him. True convenience points to the shops, which are nearer your apartment and where you get better service; but there you cannot escape that gaze, that attentiveness, which is *part* of the better service. In the department store, you glide in and immediately the dream of untroubled shopping lies all around you: a dream of perhaps buying anything, or everything, without risk, without having to spend a cent, without being reminded that you are physically there at all—you, the small creature that in shops is confounded with the rest of mortality. The shopkeeper's glance reminds you that like all his customers you are an intruder, concrete, suspect, an animal without benefit of noble dreams, at least until you have proved your superiority with hard cash.

Lans, 5/2/84

I'm starting to suffer from anxiety as to what I shall talk about to my Polish audiences next week—especially since discovering that all my notes for proper lectures were left in New York. I am supposed to lecture three times, in three cities; a fact that led me to ask my kind mentor Tomasz if I could give the same lecture on each occasion (of course *he* will be attending all three). I now realize that with or without my notes the problem lies elsewhere: partly in the expectations of my audiences—what they want to hear—and even more in what they *can* hear. I know nothing about the potential of listening in a Polish university audience, and what I imagine is certainly born of dreams of the most insubstantial kind. I can easily resolve to make the best of myself available; what I know to be my best, presented in the most effective way, may remain utterly inaudible to them. (I have no doubts as to my "visibility": but my Irish cowboy air may only persuade them to listen for a message and an attitude that I can only provide in a third-hand way—I'm thinking of the idea of America as open and direct [and of course they may *not* relish that: again, how can I know?]). Maybe I'd better read and not talk or at least read first and talk later. As usual, I want to make my appearances occasions that "work," that "produce results"; and (as usual) I have no doubts that I can make this happen. But how, but how?

Lans, 5/3/84

This morning you find yourself at a loss as you face your challenging, reassuring twenty-line preliminary to the real work of the day, not because you have nothing to write about but because you have a number of things to write about. So write about all of them, without striving after a conclusion—conclusion meaning meandering through the subject until you arrive, with some kind of "final" rhetorical effect, at your twentieth line. First, the out-of-date peculiarity you noticed in *The Marble Faun:* the unquestioned assumption that the Roman Catholic Church is corrupt and false. Hawthorne seems to be unquestioningly religious, and the self-evidence lies all on the side of New England practices or at least attitudes, even if Hilda does find relief in the confessional. What of the meagerness of New England doctrine compared to that of Rome, so full of the classical thought Hawthorne admired? Next: you have not reordered any Turkish cigarettes from Geneva, and you are actually looking forward to their running out so that you can return to your earlier and supposedly healthier habits of snuff and cigars. In the meantime you go on happily smoking your remaining cigarettes—ten to go. Next: you have, after many months of neglect, started practicing the piano regularly, following your old routine of sight-reading, finger exercises, learning and working over new pieces. Whom, in your heart of hearts, do you expect to play them for? Last: what subject (or subjects) never enters these pages at all unless through allusion or masked? You wonder if this exclusion doesn't jeopardize the entire project. Will formal games imposed on your material—like writing about *le mot* and then replacing it with *la mort*—suffice to redeem this failing?

Lans, 5/4/84

Pain scares you. For the last two nights, at the moment you go to bed, "lightning" pains have flashed down the right side of your face close to your nose. Each flash passes quickly so that the pain, electrical in its impression, has left by the time you start reacting to it. Sometimes two flashes follow close on one another but, so far, never unbearably close. You're scared by the possibility of their coming in uninterrupted succession. What would that be like? Certainly not what you imagine; but it seems probable that you would find yourself reduced to simply handling the pain as best you could. Needless to say, the fright brings with it visions of a depressing eventuality: that of becoming a permanent victim of facial neuralgia (by the way, you now know why it was called "tic douloureux": twitch = flash), having to calm down that miscreant ganglion with alcohol injections or lasers that will leave half your face forever limp. You will lead a recluse's life, never going out (and when you must, masked by scarf, hat, and dark glasses), receiving your friends always in a penumbral glow. . . . You recognize this as utterly unlikely, but in the dark, enduring the flashes, this presents itself as the *only* likely outcome. All other realities—thoughts, daydreams, even your so infinitely comforting sexual daydreams—have withdrawn from your reach: you lie there only wondering if and when the next flash will skewer your right eye. If this condition takes a turn for the worse, you can perhaps best respond to it by getting out of bed, going to your desk, and writing in this book.

Lans, 5/5/84

Funk time. At least, fuck-off time. 4:30 P.M., and you're now writing these lines. . . . Furthermore, you returned from Poland ten days ago, and today for the first time you have opened these pages. (You worked some in Paris, but not much.) No doubt you have many or at least several excuses. You're depressed, physically as well as whatever the other kind of depression is called. You're newly on the wagon, and this lowers your energy for two or three days. N.'s reaction to the last chapter of *Cigarettes* disappointed you keenly and goes on discouraging you (= you go on using it to discourage yourself). Your tic douloureux in spite of all the medication hasn't improved—not painful but very much present—and today you increased your daily dose of Tegretol to six. These excuses only justify what you have done so often and are now doing once again in *slightly* novel circumstances (i.e. drowsiness, "lowered blood pressure" [almost wrote: lowered blood pleasure]). You are creating a situation in which you make yourself an object of almost continuous self reproach. Your entire life then turns into "a failure." Since you and yours are provided for, you are not sinning by sitting in the sun reading a newspaper, or "wasting time," or even, conceivably, feeling sorry for yourself because you're behaving like a schmuck. Nevertheless you insist on thinking about what you aren't doing. Why not simply do it? Will your work suffer from being undertaken in a state of dull-mindedness and discouragement? Let *it* suffer. You can meanwhile enjoy yourself. "It" is only something for you to play with, and to invite the rest of the world to join you in playing with. Keep playing yourself. It may take a little longer, since you're such a schmuck. You know that sooner or later you'll get it right, and others will come and join in the fun.

Lans, 6/1/84

Although Beata G., referring to General Jaruzelski's regime, asserted that politics affects everything, I was struck during my visit to Poland by how many acts have nothing to do with political systems. I noticed the first when I was boarding a bus in Lublin to go back to Warsaw: a girl was saying goodbye to a soldier leaving by the same bus. I could imagine no difference in what the couple was feeling or saying ("This lousy army . . .") from what such a couple would feel or say in America or France; certainly their looks and gestures were no different. The same held true for meetings of all kinds—lovers, friends, working associates. Other such acts: buying a snack in the street (*zapikanka;* hot dog; *crêpe*); windowshopping; catching buses, trolleys, planes (also reaching your seat in time for the start of a concert); getting up in the morning and going to bed at night—brushing teeth, using the john (Polish differences here observably no greater than intra-American ones). If I knew more, I could include aspects of dressing: the time spent on it, what it's supposed to mean, the Poles perhaps closer to the French than to us, but then France and Poland share a Catholic European identity, while America pretends not to be European at all. Activities where the regime makes a difference should begin with those affected by the economic situation it has created: shopping, obviously, and all the occupations dependent on what you can and cannot buy— reading no less than driving an expensive car that runs on rationed gas. I've noted these token observations not to belittle the difficulties of the Poles but to say that my sympathy with them consists not of sorrow over a pathetic plight but of a sense of identity.

Lans, 6/2/84

Today *must* go fast—you're running even later than usual. With the usual excuses, which means with excuses, some respectable, others less so. You are pleased to have finished your letter to R. about his mother's death. On Saturday (two days ago), you began making real progress with the revision of your essay on *The Duplications,* so that you can be sure of finishing it tomorrow if not today. Incidentally, remember to rejoice in the diminishing of recent pretexts for excuses: you have grown accustomed to a six-a-day dose of Tegretol, your body has recovered from abrupt alcohol withdrawal, and yesterday on the phone N. did her best to reassure you about *Cigarettes* (it's potentially marvelous or she wouldn't be bothering, it's details of execution that bother her, she can only read first drafts as if they were finished books). Will you agree to rejoice that these obstacles have been removed, that is, that you can now do exactly what you want? I agree. Will you also agree to do today what you have been postponing for three days at least, even though you know (think of the advice you give others!) that nothing but satisfaction can proceed from it; something you avoid just like every Sue and Sam because you dread the benevolent truth, and to such an extent that even though it had been your primary concern when you began writing these lines you succeeded until you were halfway through them in forgetting it (again)? In sum: take one hour, go into your center, and look at what is happening to you. I agree. (You're acting as though you were going to visit Majdanek.)

Lans, 6/4/84

It snowed again this morning, although less thickly and long than two days ago, Sunday afternoon. Monday morning the snow still lay on the ground, or rather *not* on the ground: on a month's growth of grass, substantial if retarded, and on branches that had except for those of ash and poplar put forth their mild-green leaves. Thus through the snow, filtered through its whiteness, various greens appeared, greens that I had never before seen. (I had seen snowfalls on trees in full leaf, but in September, with its darker and duller greens.) Driving down from the house on the road that overlooked the plain and hillsides exhibiting these novel colors, I tried to identify the feelings they inspired, and wondered also what feelings they *might* inspire; asking myself what, since we are obliged to have feelings about everything, does the sight of something new evoke in us, and what role is played by the awareness of newness in itself? I most certainly did not feel the melancholy exultation brought on by a "new"—yet another!—sunset; I once thought that Camus's explanation of the effect by the "variété infinie du monde" might actually mean something. I felt a pleasure in seeing something familiar unfamiliarly revealed; an anticipation of new sensations, no doubt coinciding with my decision to notice my feelings; a sense of safety—things had revealed themselves to be not at all what they seemed, which implies that familiarity serves to remind one only of the inadequacy of life. I concluded that these feelings follow on first snowfalls in any season; so the question remained—what feeling did this one, with its never-seen colors, particularly provoke? Curiosity as to what it meant.

Lans, 6/5/84

Tennis days: the French clay court championships at Roland-Garros, which for the first time I can watch at home. The prospect of domesticating this tournament, Wimbledon, and Forest Hills originally discouraged and convinced me while I was reaching a decision about buying (at last) a television set: I thought, how nice to watch tennis at home, and I thought, how much time I'll waste watching tennis at home. The result has turned out better than I feared. I didn't tune in until the men's quarterfinals. I also acknowledged, about ten years after the fact, that watching tennis on television provides undeniable pleasure. (This week, furthermore, I'll miss the semifinals and finals because of the OuLiPo seminar at Château de Rajat.) Since acknowledging this pleasure I notice how much more pleasurable it has become. Before, when I felt remorse at not doing something "better," I tended to involve myself in the matches as if they were matters of life and death (whose, I wonder?), or at least of violence and pain. I still take sides now, almost automatically for whoever is behind (something not automatic in other sports: I hoped the Tigers this year would go on to a 50-5 won and lost record so that I could abound in their superiority). If I still like to take sides, it's chiefly to make the match I'm watching more interesting (entertaining). I didn't feel yesterday that Arias had been humiliated by McEnroe, or Carlsson by Gomez. McEnroe's mastery has to do only with the ball and the court. Carlsson's ebullience right down to the last point had nothing to do with bravery unjustly vanquished; it was a joy in itself (not for him, I guess, but who knows?). Why ever hesitate to recognize the beauty of athletes?

Lans, 6/6/84

When you go to piss in the bathroom with people within possible earshot (and sometimes with no people around at all), you direct your jet at the edge of the pool of water in the toilet bowl so as to reduce the noise you make. (Long ago you observed that peeing on the enamel of the bowl splashed a spray over its edges—something even less nice than making a watery racket.) You are astonished when other men disappear into the bathroom and immediately produce the almost roaring sound of drilled water that you so anxiously avoid, pissing happily, or at least with no audible sign of hesitation, straight into the center of the pool, its deepest and so loudest point. You notice that your astonishment contains no trace of disapproval. You not only take no offense at the undisguised noise you hear, you even feel a certain admiration and respect for its instigator, like those a timid little boy feels for a confident grown-up. Perhaps your admiration is centered on this man's so surely knowing that his behavior has no relevance to people's opinion of him—he knows that no one cares whether he is pissing or not, openly or not, because everybody does it, and does it in the knowledge that they are practicing a universal act. This knowledge has somehow escaped you. What exactly have you imagined in its place?

Lans, 6/12/84

(To continue): You have no ready answer to the last question. You know, however, that the answer or answers will touch on all the mechanisms you cling to in order to justify your reticence before life: reticence originally conceived of as retention—proved as recently as your Polish trip, when you avoided taking a shit when the act might appear (sounds, smells!) semipublic. Taken to an extreme you have never yet reached, this inclination would lead you to prefer pain to revealing the embarrassment of the source of pain, as if that must necessarily be interpreted as a failing on your part. This behavior conceivably reveals pride: not to admit that ordinary responses to ordinary "problems" are ordinarily yours. You should, therefore you can behave better than that. Something else is also going on, something connected (as in your father) with the predilection for privacy; and privacy differs from solitude. This has led you to live at the end of a dwindling road past a hamlet that lies beyond an out-of-the-way village in a country not your own. It led you, out of the awareness that you could hardly stand writing about common human passions, to discover ways of writing in which the lives around you could be ignored and your own dealt with only indirectly. This might be called pride but it is better called terror. Even now when you know that you have no one to be terrified of, you conserve the habits of flight. You still have not answered the question, what is it you imagine (in place of the knowledge that has escaped you)? The question perhaps can never be answered except through psychoanalysis or poetry. It lies in a world beyond recall because you cannot dare recall it.

Lans, 6/13/84

You would not tolerate such habits of flight (of retention, of withdrawal, to use at last a word with overt sexual overtones, or undertones, although you know, even if you haven't thought about it in this connection, how thoroughly your sexuality is implicated in everything you have been saying), you would not tolerate such habits in a student or a friend. You would reassure and berate them in a mock-stern, perfectly serious, and occasionally productive way, so clearly to you would appear the waste of themselves they are indulging in. You would not tell them "do this, do that" but lure them towards choosing, in a domain both essential and not overly frightening, some mode of action from which they had refrained (something a little more committed than pissing loudly in a toilet bowl). You might point out opportunities already present in their lives for getting involved, for getting out of their "privacy" or whatever form their "it sounds great but I can't do it"-ness might take. And then, when they took the little leap, they would discover that they were not losing but gaining something, and the something gained might be called themselves. Now you must be beginning to realize from what I have been telling you that you are indulging in foolishness not to benefit from your own perceptiveness in this respect. Plainly you need to establish a way—or better, ways—for communicating with (not yourself but) you-stuck-in-a-situation, such as the present situation of flight. As one way, you can always choose to go into your center—there, the other day, you met T. and learned that if your trigeminal neuralgia had anything to do with suppressing something, the thing suppressed could only be yourself. She told you that in this matter you should have no concern for anyone else, only for your own fullness, the wonderful, happy, powerful fullness you were so imperfectly realizing. Notice that since then you haven't gone back to find out how to do this.

Lans, 6/14/84

Your behavior might be said to rely on the idea of conservation. You are motivated by a fear of having something important to lose. You hold back, you avoid risk, you postpone acts of generosity until you know your safety is assured. At the same time, you realize that you have nothing to conserve (except your "chains"), nothing to lose, nothing that openness will endanger. In spite of your knowledge, your goals incline towards isolation and chastity, whereas you know that involvement and sexual liveliness can show up anxieties as fictions. Somewhat more positively, your inclinations express themselves in getting done whatever you have agreed with yourself should be done. This checklist attitude hardly liberates you. Yesterday you had a demonstration of the fact. You did everything you had planned (except for one item—practicing the piano—that lay outside your commitments to your work and those you love). At the end of the day, a day of inspiring beauty, so fair you were able to let down the drawbridge in your study and bring the summer woodland into your workspace, you became irritable, petulant, closed off from those around you. Doing what you had set out to do had brought you little satisfaction, because the achievement was dedicated to some superstitious rite such as "performance of duty," not to recreating your wholeness, which would have turned you towards sharing, towards supporting others, towards play. You used to garden the same way: you made weeding an act of cleaning up, not of encouraging growth. Such acts in every case deny the present and attempt an almost helpless expiation of something deep in the past: something unreal because imagined by one who no longer exists, and who, if he did exist, would know even less than the actual you the difference between his ass and a hole in the ground—a strange model to emulate now.

Lans, 6/15/84

Are you going to wait until you are on the point of death to give up this model: your old, old self, tiny, terrified, aware of his power only through the intensity of the anxieties that shriveled him? A lifetime of refusal ending in a revelation that melts the past in one moment or movement of surrender to the truth makes a fit drama for literature, as you just rediscovered in finishing *The Book of Ebenezer Le Page.* The copiousness of your tears (as you the "modernist" abounded in the "romanticism" of Ebenezer's last pages) suggests the intensity with which you deny yourself the process of opening-up that so touched you in that imaginary old man. Why else were you crying? What burial were you mourning over, if not that of your own unrealized life? Art gives you such a lovely excuse for this self-indulgence, like the nineteenth-century bourgeois of Paris and Milan weeping at *La Traviata!* Here of course the question of your own work returns to trouble you, and you ask: "Aren't my last two novels cop-outs, too?" Not with the tight-lipped reticence of *The Conversions* and *Tlooth,* but in the way their austerity gives way at the end to one great burst of feeling (Twang's last letter, the passionate friendship of Maud and Elizabeth). Doesn't this remind you of works like Bergman's *The Virgin Spring?*—sentimental abdications that relegate the problem-opportunities of life to a domain of general wishfulness (whether of mystical belief or of hope-against-hope), leaving out all the loony and lively moments in our groping, step-by-step lives that offer us the real if difficult occasions of revelation? "Only fools want to reach conclusions"—and such outbursts of feeling in their solitary abandon provide a conclusion of sorts, even if a remarkably vague one. You should be willing to accept—as you so often have taught—not knowing where you're going. After all, you don't.

Lans, 6/16/84

The temptation: to have a few conclusions stored away that you can take out when needed; that is, all the time. A very ordinary kind of conclusion you use: do the good duty of getting done what you're supposed to during the day. You will then have a reason to give yourself the reward of wine at evening. Once again, you recognize your father: you can see him in you, sitting down with his glass, settling down into self-gratification; everything must now suit the justly rewarded man's whim. You can hardly be called an alcoholic. You can admit, however, that even in the earliest moments of the day you will think of this reward, of the time when you can stop paying attention and let yourself go. You would do better letting yourself go during the rest of the day and, when evening came and you drank your wine, using it as a chosen opportunity to play games with those you love, bringing your knowledge of the day with you, dancing with it across the quirky gaps that drinking unexpectedly discloses. Why, during your daytime pursuits, try to conclude, to close in on yourself when you can't possibly succeed at it? Not unless you agree to play dead, which is mortifying (NB etymology) for you and enough of a trial to those around you to make them sometimes want to cry (they don't dare kick your ass)? Consider the past two-and-a-half weeks, during which you haven't drunk at all. After a first few days of physical letdown (which you could avoid if you had the confidence not to resort to all-or-nothingness) and a few moments of sundown longing since then, you have spent your evenings well and happily. (You did smoke a little grass at cocktail time, but—something new for you—you learned how to function alertly with it.) You know that no part of you has been lost—no mechanism of consolation or respite or reinvigoration. You have been completely there all the time, and you have realized, again, that you have no place to go except where you are, and that that place, changing from one second to the next, is no smaller than the universe. Is that too big for you? Make up a new one. In every case, it will be all yours.

Lans, 6/18/84

Since you came to Paris yesterday, you have submitted your afflicted parts—trigeminal nerve and left knee—to the consideration of specialists. They gave you professional advice: what you were paying for, not really what you wanted. You wanted to be given a super remedy for low blood pressure and to have your knee fingered back into painless normality. Instead, you got the news that your blood pressure is normal and a nice massage of your knee, together with the advice to take it easy, since the tendons of the meniscus need time to recover. You began drinking wine again, not because of any of this but because you had surpassed the weight loss you'd set as a goal twenty days ago (7 kilos or 15 lbs.). You enjoyed drinking an excellent Sancerre (and at lunch a Tavel), although the effect fell short of expectations. Tegretol must be identified as the spoiler. What a blessing Tegretol will be if it encourages you to remain in a state of self-awareness and self-regeneration by depriving you of your habitual drop-out technique! Notice how your two non-productive habits—holding yourself back because you're afraid of losing something and going unconscious through swigging wine—mutually maintain each other. One way this works: in wine, you do and say silly things, and you also can't remember things (silly or not). This "looks like" letting go and can be used to justify holding back. Just like the end of the zip-line—you let go and broke the rules and were swamped in punishing shame, leading to: "I'll always be a fuck-up!" Poor baby!

Paris, 6/20/84

And so, coming to Venice, you have learned a little more about loss—what you've lost or feel you've lost, what you think you are afraid to lose. You remember how, when you lived here, your feelings on returning to this city shifted from an exaltation full of desire (particularly desire of discovery) to pleasure in coming back to a nice place where you lived. At the time, you experienced this shift as welcome. In fact, achieving it struck you, with a little hindsight, as one of the reasons for living in Venice: you had succeeded in ridding yourself of a longing that was almost suffocating in its intensity, not so much by investigating or satisfying it as by wearing it down. Now, during your first days back, you suffer from precisely that loss, with a sadness that usually makes you physically ill: you have lost that bewilderment of desire. You no longer walk through the streets in a state of wild expectation that has the precise colors of Venetian stone, water, and sky—all, at certain hours, the same giddy and heartrending pink, of all things!—an expectation that could only vaguely point to what it sought. You knew this city as the place of desire that has no goal: of desire itself. You can hardly bear thinking that you have given that up. Venice has been turned into a sepulchre. What else can it be, since the world can be represented as desire or as desire lost, perhaps even as both, but never as anything else? Someone is buried here—a blond-haired child, wanting this and that, wanting everything. You still want those things but now know they will be denied him, because he has been buried here alive, and you only go on moping over him instead of doing what you can to set him free.

Venice, 6/25/84

You've come to the end of your pad. You will be giving up your twenty-line warm-up sessions for the time being, at least until you buy another pad. The sessions served their first purpose, which aimed at getting you past the illusory and no less discouraging obstacle to writing that is created by the fear of beginnings. They may have helped in other ways. Some of them allowed you to write in modes that you might not otherwise have chosen. Some showed that you could write phrases, even sentences (and more?) off the top of your head without feeling the need to disparage and then completely rewrite them. Perhaps you should make this your next project for daily use: to find some kind of format that would oblige you to write well from the very start, the way G. wrote, after reflection and without hesitation. Now, however, you will face another aspect of G., and it's appropriate that the pad has run out at this moment, so that you can turn to this new assignment (a fitting name for the task): you have agreed to write a few pages about your friendship with him. Last year at this time you were writing your encyclopedia article about him, a difficult and painful chore. This undertaking should prove less painful (a second year has passed since he died), and it should also bring the excitement of exploring a new manner of using memory and the written word, in addition to the excitement of rediscovering a friendship that, in spite of its calamitous interruption, was one of the fullest sources of happiness in your life. It is still that—or is it? Perhaps in another way? The question still itches: can one be the friend of someone dead? You used to assert categorically that one couldn't; now you are less sure. You are about to find out the answer.

Venice, 6/26/84

Notes

	A.P., André	André Perli, our caretaker in Lans.
	D.K., David K.	David Kalstone, whom we visited in Venice each summer.
	E., Emilie	Emilie Chaix, Marie Chaix's eldest daughter, then fourteen years old.
	G., G.P., Georges	Georges Perec.
	Léo	Léonore Chaix, Marie Chaix's younger daughter, then nine years old.
	M.C., Marie	Marie Chaix.
	N., Niki	Niki de Saint Phalle, to whom I was married from 1949 to 1960.
	P., Philip	My son by Niki de Saint Phalle.
p. 12	I.C.	Italo Calvino, whom I had heard lecture at NYU.
p. 24	Martine	Martine Gandy (now Bonnet-Merle), our cleaning woman.
p. 25	"Cinq jours," etc.	"Only five days!" "Well, it's not a registered letter."
	L. and L.	Laura and Laurent Condominas, my daughter and son-in-law.
	P.O.L.	Paul Otchakovsky-Laurens, a friend who is also my French publisher.
p. 33	Fayollats	Joseph and Marie Fayollat, our neighbors in Lans.
p. 46	*La Disparition*	A novel by Georges Perec written without using any word containing the letter *e*.
p. 59	*Essayer,* etc.	The scrupulous attempt to preserve something, to make something last.
p. 70	Roger B.	The leader of the Action and Advanced Action Workshops that I took in 1983. The workshops, created by Fernando Flores and Werner Erhard, define and explore "performative speech," that is, speech capable of producing unquestionable results.
p. 72	"ces petits," etc.	These little toes that give you such a big pain.
	R.Q.	Raymond Queneau
p. 73	OuLiPo	The Ouvroir de littérature potentielle, a Paris-based group of writers and mathematicians,

founded in 1961 by Raymond Queneau and François LeLionnais for the study of "constrictive form." I became a member in 1972.

p. 75   "Le temps," etc.   Time is money. *Being on time* is the prime attribute of *the conscientious worker.* You will notice that it's the same ones who are always late.

p. 79   Villard   Villard-de-Lans, a small town six miles from our village, where Emilie went to high school.

p. 95   François L.L.   François LeLionnais, co-founder of the OuLiPo (see note to p. 73). Towards the end of the war, after many months in a concentration camp, he escaped from a prisoner convoy with two others who had "entrusted their lives to him."

p. 101   *L'hiver,* etc.   Winter has died buried in snow; the white hives have been burned . . . (from Apollinaire's "La Chanson du Mal-aimé").

p. 104   The Lot   A department in southern France where Marie's cousin Annie Auzanneau lives.

p. 107   Stade de Neige   Snow stadium: the name given to the complex of ski slopes above Lans.

p. 115   BHV, Bon Marché   The Bazar de l'Hôtel de Ville, Au Bon Marché: Parisian department stores.

p. 116   Tomasz   Tomasz Mirkowicz, who organized my visit to Poland.

p. 121   Majdanek   A Nazi concentration camp outside Lublin.

p. 122   "variété," etc.   "The world's infinite variety."

p. 126   T.   Tina Packer, a trusted friend.

p. 130   the zip-line   An exercise done during a week-long training course. It requires jumping from a considerable height; the jumper holds on to a T-bar suspended from a cable that leads to lower ground. During my descent my terror had given way to such exuberance that I forgot to follow the simple instruction not to let go of the T-bar after landing, thus creating much unnecessary work for our handlers and leaving the trainee behind me dangling in midair.

Dalkey Archive Paperbacks

DA1   **SPLENDIDE-HÔTEL**—*Gilbert Sorrentino*
Afterword by Robert Creeley
(ISBN: 0-916583-01-5, $3.95)

DA2   **SEASON AT COOLE**—*Michael Stephens*
Afterword by Thomas McGonigle
(ISBN: 0-916583-03-1, $4.50)

DA3   **CADENZA**—*Ralph Cusack*
Afterword by Gilbert Sorrentino
(ISBN: 0-916583-05-8, $4.50)

DA4   **WALL TO WALL**—*Douglas Woolf*
(ISBN: 0-916583-07-4, $4.50)

DA5   **IMPOSSIBLE OBJECT**—*Nicholas Mosley*
(ISBN: 0-916583-09-0, $4.50)

DA6   **ACCIDENT**—*Nicholas Mosley*
Afterword by Steven Weisenburger
(ISBN: 0-916583-11-2, $4.50)

DA7   **OUT OF FOCUS**—*Alf MacLochlainn*
(ISBN: 0-916583-13-9, $4.50)

DA8   **SOME INSTRUCTIONS TO MY WIFE**—*Stanley Crawford*
(ISBN: 0-916583-15-5, $4.50)

DA9   **TOO MUCH FLESH AND JABEZ**—*Coleman Dowell*
(ISBN: 0-916583-21-X, $8.00)

DA10 **HE WHO SEARCHES**—*Luisa Valenzuela*
Translated by Helen Lane
(ISBN: 0-916583-20-1, $8.00)

DA11 **OUR SHARE OF TIME**—*Yves Navarre*
Translated by Dominic Di Bernardi and Noëlle Domke
(ISBN: 0-916583-28-7, $9.95)

DA12 **PIERROT MON AMI**—*Raymond Queneau*
Translated by Barbara Wright, Afterword by Inez Hedges
(ISBN: 0-916583-40-6, $7.95)

DA13 **20 LINES A DAY**—*Harry Mathews*
(ISBN: 0-916583-41-4, $7.95)

DA14 **CONTACT HIGHS: Selected Poems 1957-1987**—*Alan Ansen*
Introduction by Steven Moore, Afterword by Rachel Hadas
(ISBN: 0-916583-45-7, $11.95)

DA15 **WILLIE MASTERS' LONESOME WIFE**—*William H. Gass*
(ISBN: 0-916583-46-5, $7.95)

For a complete catalog of our titles, or to order any of these books, write to Dalkey Archive Press, 1817 79th Avenue, Elmwood Park, IL 60635. One book, 10% off; two books or more, 20% off; add $3.00 postage and handling.